Readers' Favorite ®
Book Reviews and Award Contest

2024 INTERNATIONAL BOOK AWARDS
In recognition of excellence in writing

Silver Medal Winner
Non-Fiction - Gov/Politics

Undermining the U.S. Constitution

Diane S. Vann

Congratulations on your award!

The Readers' Favorite Team

Undermining the U.S. Constitution
Diane Vann
Reviewed by Reyan Boris Mishra

Are you well-versed in U.S. history and the Constitution, or do you just know the basics? No matter where you stand on the interest-in-politics scale, the book in question is in all probability going to leave you with food for thought. Undermining The U.S. Constitution pits the Communist Manifesto against the U.S. Constitution, and explores the consequences and repercussions of fanning communism, also known as Marxism.

The author, Diane S. Vann, recounts her experience as an Army Nurse and how she understood the threat posed by communism. Not only does she talk about the Communist Manifesto and its impacts, but she also discusses the ways the country can get rid of communism and ensure growth for all. She compares the spread of communism in the U.S. with cancer in a patient's body. As strong as her ideologies sound, you would be surprised to see how convincingly she has put up the debate.

A variety of often-misunderstood topics are described in a detailed manner including different kinds of socialism, sustainable development, and the standpoint of active parties. In addition, one-third of the book details former President, Barack Obama's role in furthering communism across the United States. The author writes

UNDERMINING THE U.S. CONSTITUTION

HOW THE COMMUNIST MANIFESTO OF 1848 BLUEPRINTS
THE ACTIONS OF THE DEMOCRATIC PARTY

DIANE S. VANN

Copyright © 2024 by Diane S. Vann

ISBN: 978-1-998784-88-2 (Paperback)

        978-1-998784-89-9 (Hardback)

        978-1-998784-90-5 (E-book)

BOOKSIDE Press

BookSide Press
877-741-8091
www.booksidepress.com
orders@booksidepress.com

Contents

in a very matter-of-the-fact manner, and her style helps emboss her ideas. Simply put, you don't need to read between the lines. Every chapter adds a layer of reason to the author's agenda in favor of upholding the U.S. Constitution against all odds.

The interesting analogies she has used make it easy for even a layman to understand the topics effortlessly. Additionally, the backing of details with interesting, lesser-known facts and figures solidifies the core of the book. It's a book for everyone who's interested in understanding the state of the United States from an against-communism point of view. It's important to note that the author doesn't seek to change your opinion about anything. However, she mentions her experiences and analysis in such a convincing manner that you can't help rethinking what your views on the subjects are.

If you're looking for your next read, we suggest you give Undermining The U.S. Constitution a shot. It's sure to provide you with some interesting insights about the politics of the United States. Whether one agrees with her conclusions or not, Vann's book is an invitation to engage in a critical conversation about the state of the Constitution in America. If you haven't yet explored books having to do with politics, this book is a good place to test whether the genre is up your alley.

Undermining the U.S. Constitution
Diane Vann
Reviewed by Mark Heisey

"The call is out now for the silent majority of taxpaying, hardworking Americans to become politically active without delay."

America was founded on the principles and ideas that the original planners laid out in the Declaration of Independence and the Constitution of the United States. One of the results is that capitalism is a major component and driving force in how America operates. Communism directly opposes capitalism's view that hard work leads to wealth which leads to owning property and improving one's position in society. Communism directly opposes private property ownership and working to make money for someone else, hoping that one day excess wages will allow the individual to get into a position where they can own a company and have others work for them. Communists see the working class as mere property for the wealthy elite who hoard all the best for themselves and want only the minimum necessary for the masses to keep a workforce generating income and goods for the wealthy. Clashes between these two ideologies often play out on a global scale. However, many Americans who are not political centrists but fall on the further extremes of the two parties often use these ideologies to attack their political opposites. Those far on the

Republican path tend to see Democrats as elite communists who want a one-world government meant to cater to the elites. In contrast, some Democrats see Republicans as authoritarian and tyrannical. Each group continually claims that they represent the silent majority.

In her thought-provoking work, Vann argues that Democrats have been actively pursuing a communist plan for decades and that the average American needs to wake up before it is too late to stop the nation from turning into a communist country. Vann points out various decisions and actions by political leaders to support this thesis. One that stands out is Agenda 21, nicknamed "The Communist Manifesto of 1992." Vann talks about how this agreement, made by the United Nations and signed by representatives of 178 countries, including Republican President George H.W. Bush, is actively taking communism globally. She cites the Freedom Advocates online as pointing out how Mexico, Canada, and the United States are all part of this communist action from 1992, which looks to economically equalize these three countries and use NGOs (non-governmental organizations) to depopulate rural America and give all that property to the central authority. Additionally, Vann goes through a timeline of the actions of former President Barack Obama, a Democrat, and illustrates how various decisions taken during his presidency can be directly tied to The Communist Manifesto, a book written in 1848 by Karl Marx and Friedrich Engels, which talked directly about class struggles, social classes, production, and private property.

Vann's writing is clear and well-researched. It is easy to follow her logic and see the ties she draws between current issues/leaders and communist texts and ideas. She uses simple sentence structure and basic language to put forth her thoughts on complex issues in understandable and easy-to-absorb arguments. The author's work joins the plethora of books from both ends of the political spectrum currently being published that reference the silent majority as supporting a particular view, unveiling the increasing divisiveness within society. This book will undoubtedly provoke a lot of deep discussions and will likely appeal especially to those who share similar political views as those expressed in the text.

2024 Pacific Book Awards
In recognition of excellence in writing

Winner - Best Current Events & Politics

Undermining the U.S. Constitution

By: Diane S. Vann

Congratulations on your award!

Nicole Sorkin

Nicole Sorkin, President

The Pacific Book Awards Team

Undermining the U.S. Constitution
Diane Vann
Reviewed by Irene Jacobs

Diane S. Vann's Undermining the U.S. Constitution offers a critical analysis of the parallel universe between political principles and ideologies. Vann navigates the worlds of politics, philosophy, and history to illuminate the intersection between the foundational principles of the U.S. Constitution and the principles set forth in the Communist Manifesto. Throughout the pages, readers are guided through an exploration of how the Democratic Party's actions are allegedly influenced by the ideological underpinnings of the 1848 Manifesto.

With meticulous research and analysis, the author presents a narrative which challenges conventional perspectives on the Democratic Party's alignment with historical ideologies. Undermining the U.S. Constitution engages readers in a thought-provoking journey, encouraging them to reconsider the political landscape through a lens which intertwines the past and present. A chronological examination of events, ideas, and political shifts guides the reader through the book's systematic structure. Commendation is warranted for the meticulous presentation of evidence within the work. A wide array of historical documents, quotations, and references are drawn upon to substantiate claims, enhancing the credibility of the arguments. The utilization of primary sources provides readers with a tangible connection to the historical context explored. The author's perspective is evident throughout the book, and Vann's background adds weight to the analysis.

The writing style adopted by Vann is straightforward, making complex ideas understandable to a broad audience. The book excels in conveying intricate political concepts without sacrificing clarity, contributing to its readability and engagement. Furthermore, the relevance of Vann's arguments to contemporary political discourse is a notable aspect. The connection of historical events to present-day political discussions is effectively established, underscoring the enduring impact of ideologies on American politics. However, the work is observed to lean towards a particular viewpoint, prompting questions about objectivity. While the passion for the subject is palpable, a more nuanced exploration of opposing perspectives is suggested to strengthen the overall argument.

In conclusion, Undermining the U.S. Constitution by Diane S. Vann is a thought-provoking exploration of the alleged influence of the Communist Manifesto on the Democratic Party. Strengths lie in the meticulous use of evidence, accessible writing style, and relevance to contemporary discussions. The work stands as a valuable addition to the literature on U.S. politics, inviting readers to reflect on the intricate interplay of historical ideologies and present-day political actions. This book appeals to multiple audiences because of its broad genres. It gratifies political memorandums, philosophical questions and thoughts, non-fiction enthusiasm, and historical context. All of these make the book a rich reality from which to study.

Foreword

During my travels within and outside of the United States as an Army nurse, I learned that the respect and freedom for each and every individual fostered by the U.S. Constitution written in 1787 results in their achieving unlike anywhere else in the world. I also learned that some do not appreciate that respect and freedom for others nor those results, their beliefs and values are more in line with those expressed in the Communist Manifesto written later in 1848. Because the protections given by the U.S. Constitution extend to all, its opponents within and outside of the United States will never cease to exist. Therefore its supporters must always be prepared and able to defend it.

The content in my 2012 first edition remains with the number of pages more than doubled. The latest added is Socialism/Communism STATUS CODE RED. In it I list the insidious changes already made by Socialists/Communists/Globalists in the United States and their current plans for Environmental, Social, and Governance (ESG) and Transhumanism. A compilation of my observations and references for the reader's further self education, I wrote this book for all people who do not want a one world government that treats them like animals.

Communist Manifesto Opposes Constitution

The Constitution was the result of the maturing of the thoughts and ideas put forward by many different outstanding people. They were people with varying levels of education, who knew from experience what they did not want in government. They knew what it was like to have their hopes and dreams limited by the social status of their birth and by the intrusion of government.

After rejecting England's monarch, our founding fathers "brain stormed" together on what government would work best for all people. Their ideas centered on their shared belief in the existence of a power greater than them. In the Declaration of Independence they asserted that all men are created equal and endowed by their Creator with unalienable rights neither transferable to nor deniable by man. After weighing pros and cons for a democracy or a republic, they chose the republic. A pure democracy is government by the majority (or mob rule) while a republic is government that protects the minority from the majority.

Practical experience came from the implementation in 1781 of the first Constitution, the Articles of Confederation. The second and final Constitution, signed by 39 delegates on September 17, 1787, delineated a representative republic with three branches of government (legislative, executive, and judicial) and an amendment process. The amendment process, the "living part" of the Constitution, alters the Constitution when needed but never erases it. Added to the Constitution in 1868, the 14th Amendment resulted in the expectation of equal and impartial justice under the law.

The Constitution places ultimate power in the hands of the voters rather than the elected. It protects our individual rights. Following the Constitution made the United States of America the primary leader of the free world. Our nation has prospered and been blessed by God. When called upon by other nations in wars or famines, we helped them.

The United States of America (USA), because of the Constitution, nurtures what Karl Marx called "capitalism," where private individuals and corporations invest in and own the means of production and distribution rather than government. Capitalism produces competition that breeds the incentive to be creative and improve things. Individuals in the USA have the freedom to choose what they will do; for example, one can choose to spend one's life working to accumulate money or working as a nurse.

The Communist Manifesto was written by Karl Marx and Frederick or Friedrich Engels in 1847-8 for people who were knowledgeable about and directly opposed to America's founding fathers' beliefs and the Constitution. (Within the manifesto America is referred to five times and the word constitution is mentioned three). The manifesto is a detailed prescription for bringing down advanced countries like the USA. In brief, the prescription is for Communists of the working class to first take over a political party, gain control of the government, and then bring the ruling middle class and government down with the help of trade unions and socialists. The desired outcome of the prescription is that no class will oppress another and everyone's status will be equal, even though only the Communists will know the ultimate plan for the worldwide government. There is no further description of the future, which is left as a utopian void to be filled in by the Communists. (W. Cleon Skousen described in 1958 in his book The Naked Communist the atheistic "Communist dictatorship" that resulted in nations that followed Marx's prescription).

Andrew Jackson (1767-1845), the 7th president of the United States from 1829-37, signed into law the Indian Removal Act on May 28, 1830. The Democratic Party of the USA, the oldest existing Democratic Party in the world, was started in 1828-32 to aid in Jackson's reelection. Following his landslide reelection, Native American Indians without hope left their lands and possessions in the states of Georgia, Alabama, North Carolina, Tennessee and Texas. They were relocated to the Indian Territory (now Oklahoma— Choctaw for "red people"—state). More than 4,000 lost their lives on the "Trail of Tears." Proceeds from the sale of the Indian lands went to the federal treasury to settle the government's debt.

According to Marx and Engels in 1848, "the theory of the Communists may be summed up in the single sentence: Abolition of private property." President Jackson personified that theory when he enforced the Indian Removal Act. Their approval of Jackson's actions may be at least in part, if not all, of the reason why they wrote near the end of the Communist Manifesto that "In short, the Communists. ... labor everywhere for the union and agreement of the democratic parties of all countries." (The term democrat was used a total of three times in the Communist Manifesto: one time in "Social-Democrats;" one time in "Democratic Socialists;" and one time in "the democratic parties." All three were in the last section, Section 4).

Norman Mattoon Thomas (1884-1968), six time candidate for president of the United States, reportedly said in a speech in 1944 that "The American people will never knowingly adopt socialism. But, under the name of 'liberalism,' they will adopt every fragment of the socialist program, until one day America will be a socialist nation, without knowing how it happened." Then later he said "I no longer need to run as a Presidential Candidate for the Socialist Party. The Democrat Party has adopted our platform."

The Democratic Socialists of America (DSA) is the United States (U.S.) democratic socialist organization affiliated with the Socialist International. The Socialist International is a federation of democratic socialist, social democratic, social progressive, labor parties and organizations. In October 2009, the DSA released a newsletter listing 70 members of the 111th U.S. Congress as DSA members. All but Senator Bernie Sanders, an Independent from Vermont, were members of the Democratic Party. All but 7 were reelected in 2010 to the 112th Congress.

The Communist Party USA officially endorsed President Barack Obama for the 2012 election on August 4, 2011.

In contrast, the Republican Party was organized in 1854-56 for opposing the extension of slavery. Abraham Lincoln (1809-1865), President of the United States (1861-65) during the Civil War, being advised by fellow Republican and former slave Frederick Douglass, issued the Emancipation Proclamation (Jan. 1, 1863) freeing all slaves in those states fighting the union. Lincoln also pressed for the 13th Amendment barring slavery forever. It was ratified and added to the Constitution on December 6, 1865 following Lincoln's April 15th assassination.

Today the Democratic Party is expert in distracting Americans from its historical and current actions by projecting them onto the Republican Party. Their "devious manipulation" of history and language in regard to black Americans is well documented in the 2011 book Frederick Douglass Republicans: The Movement to Re-Ignite America's Passion for Liberty by K. Carl Smith with his brother Dr. Karnie C. Smith, Sr.

The Real Communist Threat Witnessed

MY EXPERIENCE IN COMMUNIST EAST BERLIN & FREE WEST BERLIN IN 1977

I am a Vietnam era veteran, and I was last posted as a registered nurse on active duty in the United States Army Reserve Nurse Corps to 2nd General Hospital, Landstuhl, Germany in 1975. During our orientation we were asked to visit East Germany (the German Democratic Republic or GDR) because Communists were telling East Germans that the American military were leaving West Germany (the Federal Republic of Germany or FRG). We were told to "wear your uniform so you will not be shot as a spy."

When World War II ended in Europe in 1945, Germany was split from north to south. The capital Berlin fell to the east of the new boundary also known as (AKA) the "Iron Curtain." Too important to cede to one side, Berlin was split into four occupied sectors. The American, British, and French sectors (AKA West Berlin) were administered by the Allies on a rotating basis. The Soviet sector (AKA East Berlin) was administered by the Soviet Union.

So in July of 1977, shortly before I was due to come home, I flew 100 miles behind the Iron Curtain to West Berlin. After finding a place to stay and touring West Berlin, I toured East Berlin by bus and then by foot via Checkpoint Charlie. After a few days I departed West Berlin on the "troop train," an overnight trip that took 9 hours because every 20 miles the train was stopped for the East German engineers to be exchanged, so they could not collude and escape with the train again. So why would anyone try to escape the utopia foretold in the Communist Manifesto or Manifesto of the Communist Party?

I found West Berlin to be very upbeat with lots of people, vehicles, stores, and colorful signs in evidence. Only one building, a church, was left with its bullet ridden walls unchanged as a memorial to World War II (the Kaiser Wilhelm Memorial). I rode public transportation and was handed a leaflet advertising a Communist demonstration which I saw and photographed later.

East Berlin was a very different story. It was depressingly quiet with very few vehicles and without colorful signs. People I walked by on my solo walking tour stared without returning my smile. A memorable statue downtown was a roughly three story high, stooped over workman wearing a huge frown with a sickle on his back.

President Barack Obama's speeches as a presidential candidate reminded me of the prepared speech of the middle aged, East Berlin guide who got on my tour bus at the Communist end of Checkpoint Charlie. Obama's communist agenda matches what I heard and witnessed that day and has inspired me to write this book for my fellow noncommunist Americans.

As we drove through East Berlin's streets, still bombed out and shot up 32 years post World War II, our guide listed problems like the need for more housing that the government was going to solve. Problems that I knew were well in hand on the free West Berlin side. Her rehearsed delivery of the utopian changes to come because of government made me think that she was brain washed.

Then we stopped for a bite to eat at a small cafeteria. I, an almost 25 year old uniformed United States Army officer, was sitting at a table with a middle aged stranger. Our tour guide confidently sat down with us and began to share how much she and her family hated living in East Germany, how her children were in trouble at school because they preferred learning English to Russian as their second language, and how her husband could leave the country to attend medical conferences but they could not accompany him.

Afterwards I was thinking that she was definitely not brain washed, and I was surprised when the stranger at the table said "That is the stupidest woman you will ever meet in your life." When I asked why, he stated "Either one of us could have been a plant." He explained that in World War II he was a spy in Berlin for the Allies, and now he was on his first visit "to see the changes."

West Berlin's Overlook of the Berlin Wall

I took a picture of the other tourists already at the top and looking down, just before mounting the steps to see the Berlin Wall and beyond. What we saw was that on the East Berlin side, no one could get as close. Instead of an overlook, there was a heavily guarded no man's land.

The Berlin Wall was built in 1961 in the former Potsdamer Platz (pictured above on the side of West Berlin's overlook of the Berlin Wall) by East Germany to stop people from leaving the Communist controlled east side for the Western controlled west side. Following this paragraph are copies of my travel orders and the pictures taken with my small Kodak 110 camera on July 31-Aug 2,

1977. Their captions are the brief descriptions I wrote on their backs (Brandenburger Tor is the German name for the Brandenburg Gate).

Front of Military Orders

TRAVEL INSTRUCTIONS   ORDRE DE ROUTE   КОМАНДИРОВКА

SWANSON DIANE E   1 LT USAR

will proceed without restriction to and from Berlin in
connection with the occupation of Berlin.

se rendra/rendront à Berlin et en reviendra/reviendront, sans
aucune limitation, pour des motifs afférents à l'occupation de
la ville.

проследует беспрепятственно в Берлин и обратно в связи
с оккупацией Берлина.

Valid for one round trip

Valable pour un voyage aller et retour

Действительна на одну поездку туда и обратно

from   to   Inclusive.
du   16 Jul 77   au   14 Aug 77   Inclus.
or_____   no_____   включительно.
         (date)
         (число)

Issued on   1 6 JUL 1977
Délivré le
Выдано (число)

Signature
Подпись

Title   GUY F. CARDINALLI
Qualité   COL, AGC
Звание   Asst Adjutant General

Back of Military Orders

East Berlin July '77 me Graveyard Memorial to Soviet soldiers killed in World
War II. Twin Stone Monuments to represent Soviet Red Flags

The Wall—Barbed Wire and Mine Fields—Looking Out at Berlin's Former
Potsdamer Platz from West Berlin

The Wall from West Berlin—In distance—east side—green roof of bunker where
Hitler committed suicide

The Wall West Berlin July '77

"Warning: You're Now Leaving West Berlin."
Brandenburger Tor from West July '77

West Berlin July '77 River Spree separating East & West Berlin--graves of East Germans who tried to escape across water

West Berlin Looking from Wittenburg Platz to the Kaiser Wilhelm Memorial

Brandenburger Tor built late 18th century on model of Propylaea in Athens as seen from East Berlin 2 Aug 77

East Berlin 31 July '77

Communist Demonstration Kurfürstendamm West Berlin 1 Aug '77

Aug 1, ' 77 West Berlin Polizei Kurfürstendamm Communist Demonstration

East Berlin Apartment Houses Aug '77

Checkpoint Charley from American sector Berlin Aug '77

INTRODUCTION TO THE COMMUNIST MANIFESTO

Contrary to what some people believe, Communism's threat to the United States (US) did not vanish with the disintegration of the Union of Soviet Socialist Republics (USSR). There is no excuse for willful ignorance of this fact. A quote attributed to Nikita Khrushchev, a leader of the USSR in the mid 20th century, is: "We can't expect the American People to jump from Capitalism to Communism, but we can assist their elected leaders in giving them small doses of Socialism, until they awaken one day to find that they have Communism."

*I believe that every American should read and understand the Communist Manifesto, because that knowledge is the key to our nation's long term defense. Due to its public domain status, the Communist Manifesto is not protected by copyright laws. The text of the entire pamphlet (without any prefaces and footnotes by Karl Marx and Frederick Engels) follows next in this book. To make it easier to get through, I **underline and italicize** the points I feel are most critical and add explanatory remarks in **bold Crimson Text** font.*

German members of the Communist League in England contracted in 1847 with Karl Marx to write the Communist Manifesto for them. He wrote it in the German language with input from his friend Frederick Engels. It was first published in German in England in February 1848.

Karl Marx reportedly grew up in an upper class family and was college educated in his homeland Germany (then Prussia). Forgoing a working class job, he lived off the proceeds of his incendiary Socialist writings and was driven out of Germany as well as other countries. Settling finally in England, there were times he could not leave his home because he had pawned his clothes. Born May 5, 1818, he lost his wife and children to disease and suicide before his death on March 14, 1883.

Reading Marx's prescription for bringing down an advanced capitalist country is not easy. I was tempted to rip it up the first 6 times

I read it. Also, it is not well written and for that I blame Marx and not the translators. Marx wrote under the pressure of time and probably with limited paper and ink, so most of his critical points are written in throwaway lines. Subsequent Communist writers continue to embellish on his points.

In his first section, Marx reduces all history to class warfare and details the two main classes of his (and our) day. The oppressor "ruling" class is the capitalist class which he calls the "bourgeoisie." The oppressed class is the working class which he calls the "proletarian." To be fair, his 1st section makes some valid observations about living conditions at his time, which was nearer the onset of the industrial age. In his 2nd section Marx describes the relationship of Communists to Proletarians. Communists, as a working-class party, are proletarians who "clearly understand the . . . ultimate general results of the proletarian movement . . . . summed up in the single sentence: Abolition of private property." The end of section 2 is the easiest part of the manifesto to read. There Marx numbered 1—10 ten interventions for bringing about the downfall of advanced capitalist countries. In his 3rd section, Marx does a review of the Socialist and Communist literature. He details the different Socialist parties of the day and their usefulness to Communists. In his short 4th section, Marx emphasizes that Communists should use various existing opposition parties for Communist purposes, and he calls on the democratic parties and working men of all countries to unite.

It is remarkable that Marx excluded mention of the slavery of his day, referring to it only as if it was in the distant past (i.e. **[that is]***, in the "history of all hitherto existing societies" and "in ancient Rome"). Instead he equated the oppression of the working class by the middle class to the oppression of the slave by the slave owner. He took the real life experiences of Africans sold into slavery in America and substituted the word proletarian for African and bourgeois for slave owner (e.g., "all family ties among the proletarians are torn asunder" and "bourgeois society ought long ago to have gone to the dogs through sheer idleness").*

It is also notable that Marx, after assessing all of the parties of the day in 1848, selected the democratic party to advance the Communist agenda. The Democratic Party of the USA, the oldest existing in the world, was started in 1828-32 to aid in the reelection of our 7th president, Andrew Jackson. President Andrew Jackson is infamous for enforcing the Indian Removal Act which he signed into law May 28, 1830.

Within the text of the Communist Manifesto, Marx takes positions in direct opposition to those taken by the authors of the Constitution of the United States. He is dismissive of political constitutions (e.g., "Into their place stepped free competition, accompanied by a social and political constitution adapted to it, and by the economical and political sway of the bourgeois class") and he is dismissive of family, country, law, morality and religion (e.g., "Law, morality, religion, are to him so many bourgeois prejudices"). Marx's Communist Manifesto is, essentially, the antithesis of the Constitution of the United States.

Diane Vann

From "Introduction" by Francis B. Randall, Sarah Lawrence College, page 25 of <u>The Communist Manifesto, Karl Marx and Friedrich Engels; the Revolutionary Economic, Political, and Social Treatise That Has Transfigured the World</u>:

At a time when most European countries were still ruled, or at least coruled, by kings and nobles, Marx had the vision to see that the bourgeoisie was taking over. "Bourgeoisie" had originally meant the inhabitants of cities, but by the Romantic age the term had come to mean the middle classes, whether they lived in cities or not. Businessmen from the greatest textile magnates to the smallest hole-in-the-wall shopkeepers, doctors, lawyers, teachers and other educated and professional people, all the groups that we now call "white collar workers" were part of the bourgeoisie. Marx often felt compelled to give a narrow economic definition of the **bourgeoisie**--"the owners of the means of capitalist production"--but he used the term to indicate the **middle classes as a whole.**

Preceding quote from: <u>**The Communist Manifesto, Karl Marx**</u> <u>**and Friedrich Engels; the Revolutionary Economic, Political, and**</u> <u>**Social Treatise That Has Transfigured the World,**</u> translation by Samuel Moore, edited by Joseph Katz, copyrighted 1964.

Bourgeoisie = Middle Class
Bourgeois = Person belonging to the Bourgeoisie or Middle Class

For background material read <u>**Marx for Beginners,**</u> by Rius.

THE COMMUNIST MANIFESTO

(a public domain document downloadable cost-free from Internet, 2011)

ALSO KNOWN AS (AKA) "TRASHING OF THE AMERICAN DREAM" & "KILLING THE GOOSE THAT LAID THE GOLDEN EGG"*

By Karl Marx and Frederick or Friedrich Engels

*Highlighting, Italicizing, Underlining and Notes in **Bold Text** *added by Diane Vann*

Introduction

A spectre is haunting Europe -- the specter of Communism. All the Powers of old Europe have entered into a holy alliance to exorcise this specter: Pope and Czar, Metternich and Guizot, French Radicals and German police-spies.

Where is the party in opposition that has not been decried as Communistic by its opponents in power? Where is the Opposition that has not hurled back the branding reproach of Communism, against the more advanced opposition parties, as well as against its reactionary adversaries?

Two things result from this fact.

I. Communism is already acknowledged by all European Powers to be itself a Power.

II. It is high time that Communists should openly, in the face of the whole world, publish their views, their aims, their tendencies, and meet this nursery tale of the Specter of Communism with a Manifesto of the party itself.

To this end, Communists of various nationalities have assembled in London, and sketched the following Manifesto, to be published in the English, French, German, Italian, Flemish and Danish languages.

Section I. Bourgeois and Proletarians

The *history of all hitherto existing societies is the history of class struggles.*

Freeman and slave, patrician and plebeian, lord and serf, guild-master and journeyman, in a word, *oppressor and oppressed*, stood in constant opposition to one another, carried on an uninterrupted, now hidden, now open fight, a fight that each time ended, either in a revolutionary reconstitution of society at large, or in the common ruin of the contending classes.

In the earlier epochs of history, we find almost everywhere a complicated arrangement of society into various orders, a manifold gradation of social rank. In ancient Rome we have patricians, knights, plebeians, slaves; in the Middle Ages, feudal lords, vassals, guild-masters, journeymen, apprentices, serfs; in almost all of these classes, again, subordinate gradations.

The modern bourgeois society that has sprouted from the ruins of feudal society has not done away with class antagonisms. It has but established new classes, new conditions of oppression, new forms of struggle in place of the old ones. ***Our epoch***, the epoch of the bourgeoisie, possesses, however, this distinctive feature: it has simplified the class antagonisms: Society as a whole is more and more splitting up into two great hostile camps, into ***two great classes***, directly facing each other: ***Bourgeoisie and Proletariat***.

From the serfs of the Middle Ages sprang the chartered burghers of the earliest towns. From these burgesses the first elements of the bourgeoisie were developed.

The discovery of America, the rounding of the Cape, opened up fresh ground for the rising bourgeoisie. The East-Indian and Chinese markets, the colonization of America, trade with the colonies, the increase in the means of exchange and in commodities generally, gave to commerce, to navigation, to industry, an impulse never before known, and thereby, to the revolutionary element in the tottering feudal society, a rapid development.

The feudal system of industry, under which industrial production was monopolized by closed guilds, now no longer sufficed for the growing wants of the new markets. The manufacturing system took its place. The guild-masters were pushed on one side by the manufacturing middle class; division of labor between the different corporate guilds vanished in the face of division of labor in each single workshop.

Meantime the markets kept ever growing, the demand ever rising. Even manufacture no longer sufficed. Thereupon, steam and machinery revolutionized industrial production. The place of manufacture was taken by the giant, Modern Industry, the place of the industrial middle class, by industrial millionaires, the leaders of whole industrial armies, the modern bourgeois.

Modern industry has established the world-market, for which the discovery of America paved the way. This market has given an immense development to commerce, to navigation, to communication by land. This development has, in its time, reacted on the extension of industry; and in proportion as industry, commerce, navigation, railways extended, in the same proportion the bourgeoisie developed, increased its capital, and pushed into the background every class handed down from the Middle Ages.

We see, therefore, how the modern bourgeoisie is itself the product of a long course of development, of a series of revolutions in the modes of production and of exchange.

Each step in the development of the bourgeoisie was accompanied by a corresponding political advance of that class. An oppressed class under the sway of the feudal nobility, an armed and self-governing association in the mediaeval commune; here independent urban republic (as in Italy and Germany), there taxable "third estate" of the monarchy (as in France), afterwards, in the period of manufacture proper, serving either the semifeudal or the absolute monarchy as a counterpoise against the nobility, and, in fact, corner-stone of the great monarchies in general, the bourgeoisie has at last, since the establishment of Modern Industry and of the world-market, conquered for itself, in the modern representative State, exclusive political sway. The executive of the modern State is but a committee for managing the common affairs of the whole bourgeoisie.

The bourgeoisie, historically, has played a most revolutionary part.

The bourgeoisie, wherever it has got the upper hand, has put an end to all feudal, patriarchal, idyllic relations. It has pitilessly torn asunder the motley feudal ties that bound man to his "natural superiors," and has left remaining no other nexus between man and man than naked self-interest, than callous "cash payment." It has drowned the most heavenly ecstasies of religious fervor, of chivalrous enthusiasm, of philistine sentimentalism, in the icy water of egotistical calculation. It has resolved personal worth into exchange value, and in place of the numberless and feasible chartered freedoms, has set up that single, unconscionable freedom -- **Free Trade**. In one word, for exploitation, veiled by religious and political illusions, naked, shameless, direct, brutal **exploitation**.

The bourgeoisie has stripped of its halo every occupation hitherto honored and looked up to with reverent awe. It has converted the physician, the lawyer, the priest, the poet, the man of science, into its paid wage laborers.

The bourgeoisie has torn away from the family its sentimental veil, and has reduced the family relation to a mere money relation.

The bourgeoisie has disclosed how it came to pass that the brutal display of vigor in the Middle Ages, which Reactionists so much admire, found its fitting complement in the most slothful indolence. It has been the first to show what man's activity can bring about. It has accomplished wonders far surpassing Egyptian pyramids, Roman aqueducts, and Gothic cathedrals; it has conducted expeditions that put in the shade all former Exoduses of nations and crusades.

The bourgeoisie cannot exist without constantly revolutionizing the instruments of production, and thereby the relations of production, and with them the whole relations of society. Conservation of the old modes of production in unaltered form, was, on the contrary, the first condition of existence for all earlier industrial classes. Constant revolutionizing of production, uninterrupted disturbance of all social conditions, everlasting uncertainty and agitation distinguish the bourgeois epoch from all earlier ones. All fixed, fast-frozen relations, with their train of ancient and venerable prejudices and opinions, are swept away, all new-formed ones become antiquated before they can ossify. All that is solid melts into air, all that is holy is profaned, and man is at last compelled to face with sober senses, his real conditions of life, and his relations with his kind.

The need of a constantly expanding market for its products chases the bourgeoisie over the whole surface of the globe. It must nestle everywhere, settle everywhere, establish connections everywhere.

The bourgeoisie has through its exploitation of the world-market given a cosmopolitan character to production and consumption in every country. To the great chagrin of Reactionists, it has drawn from under the feet of industry the national ground on which it stood. All old-established national industries have been destroyed or are daily being destroyed. They are dislodged by new industries, whose introduction becomes a life and death question for all civilized nations, by industries that no longer work up indigenous raw material, but raw material drawn from the remotest zones; industries whose products are consumed, not only at home, but in every quarter of the globe. In place of the old wants, satisfied by the productions of the country, we find new wants, requiring for their satisfaction the products of distant lands and climes. In place of the old local and national seclusion and self-sufficiency, we have intercourse in every direction, universal inter-dependence of nations. And as in material, so also in intellectual production. The intellectual creations of individual nations become common property. National one-sidedness and narrow-mindedness become more and more impossible, and from the numerous national and local literatures, there arises a world literature.

The bourgeoisie, by the rapid improvement of all instruments of production, by the immensely facilitated means of communication, draws all, even the most barbarian, nations into civilization. The cheap prices of its commodities are the heavy artillery with which it batters down all Chinese walls, with which it forces the barbarians' intensely obstinate hatred of foreigners to capitulate. It compels all nations, on pain of extinction, to adopt the bourgeois mode of production; it compels them to introduce what it calls civilization into their midst, i.e., to become bourgeois themselves. In one word, it creates a world after its own image.

The bourgeoisie has subjected the country to the rule of the towns. It has created enormous cities, has greatly increased the urban population as compared with the rural, and has thus rescued a considerable part of the population from the idiocy of rural life. Just as it has made the country dependent on the towns, so it has made barbarian and semi-barbarian countries dependent on the civilized ones, nations of peasants on nations of bourgeois, the East on the West.

The bourgeoisie keeps more and more doing away with the scattered state of the population, of the means of production, and of property. It has agglomerated production, and has concentrated property in a few hands. The necessary consequence of this was political centralization. Independent, or but loosely connected provinces, with separate interests, laws, governments and systems of taxation, became lumped together into one nation, with one government, one code of laws, one national class-interest, one frontier and one customs-tariff. The bourgeoisie, during its rule of scarce one hundred years, has created more massive and more colossal productive forces than have all preceding generations together. Subjection of Nature's forces to man, machinery, application of chemistry to industry and agriculture, steam-navigation, railways, electric telegraphs, clearing of whole continents for cultivation, canalization of rivers, whole populations conjured out of the ground -- what earlier century had even a presentiment that such productive forces slumbered in the lap of social labor?

We see then: the means of production and of exchange, on whose foundation the bourgeoisie built itself up, were generated in feudal society. At a certain stage in the development of these means of production and of exchange, the conditions under which feudal society produced and exchanged, the feudal organization of agriculture and manufacturing industry, in one word, the *feudal relations of property* became no longer compatible with the already developed productive forces; they became so many fetters. They had to be burst asunder; they were *burst asunder.*

Into their place stepped free competition, accompanied by a social and political constitution adapted to it, and by the economical and political sway of the bourgeois class.

A similar movement is going on before our own eyes. Modern bourgeois society with its relations of production, of exchange and of property, a society that has conjured up such gigantic means of production and of exchange, is like the sorcerer, who is no longer able to control the powers of the nether world whom he has called up by his spells. For many a decade past the history of industry and commerce is but the history of the revolt of modern productive forces against modern conditions of production, against the property relations that are the conditions for the existence of the bourgeoisie and of its rule. It is enough to mention the commercial ***crises*** that by their periodical return put on its trial, each time more threateningly, the existence of the entire bourgeois society. In these ***crises*** a great part not only of the existing products, but also of the previously created productive forces, are periodically destroyed. In these ***crises*** there breaks out an epidemic that, in all earlier epochs, would have seemed an absurdity -- the epidemic of over-production. Society suddenly finds itself put back into a state of momentary barbarism; it appears as if a famine, a universal war of devastation had cut off the supply of every means of subsistence; industry and commerce seem to be destroyed; and why? Because there is too much civilization, too much means of subsistence, too much industry, too much commerce. The productive forces at the disposal of society no longer tend to further the development of the conditions of bourgeois property; on the contrary, they have become too powerful for these conditions, by which they are fettered, and so soon as they overcome these fetters, they bring disorder into the whole of bourgeois society, endanger the existence of bourgeois property. The conditions of bourgeois society are too narrow to comprise the wealth created by them. And how does the bourgeoisie get over these ***crises***? On the one hand enforced destruction of a mass of productive forces; on the other, by the conquest of new markets, and by the more thorough exploitation of the old ones. That is to say, by paving the way for more extensive and more destructive *__crises__*, and by diminishing the means whereby *__crises__* are prevented.

__The weapons with which the bourgeoisie felled feudalism to the ground are now turned against the bourgeoisie itself.__

But *__not only has the bourgeoisie forged the weapons that bring death to itself; it has also called into existence the men who are to wield those weapons -- the modern working class -- the proletarians.__*

__In proportion as the bourgeoisie, i.e., capital, is developed, in the same proportion is the proletariat, the modern working class, developed -- a class of laborers, who live only so long as they find work, and who find work only so long as their labor increases capital.__ These laborers, who must sell themselves piece-meal, are a commodity, like every other article of commerce, and are consequently exposed to all the vicissitudes of competition, to all the fluctuations of the market.

Proletariat includes illegal immigrants, speech/English challenged, and others brought down, but not the non working poor.

Owing to the extensive use of machinery and to division of labor, the work of the proletarians has lost all individual character, and consequently, all charm for the workman. He becomes an appendage of the machine, and it is only the most simple, most monotonous, and most easily acquired knack, that is required of him. Hence, the cost of production of a workman is restricted, almost entirely, to the means of subsistence that he requires for his maintenance, and for the propagation of his race. But the price of a commodity, and therefore also of labor, is equal to its cost of production. In proportion therefore, as the repulsiveness of the work increases, the wage decreases. Nay more, in proportion as the use of machinery and division of labor increases, in the same proportion the burden of toil also increases, whether by prolongation of the working hours, by increase of the work exacted in a given time or by increased speed of the machinery, etc.

Modern industry has converted the little workshop of the patriarchal master into the great factory of the industrial capitalist. Masses of laborers, crowded into the factory, are organized like soldiers. As privates of the industrial army they are placed under the command of a perfect hierarchy of officers and sergeants. ***Not only are they slaves of the bourgeois class,*** and of the bourgeois State; they are daily and hourly enslaved by the machine, by the over-looker, and, above all, by the individual bourgeois manufacturer himself. The more openly this despotism proclaims gain to be its end and aim, the more petty, the more hateful and the more embittering it is.

The less the skill and exertion of strength implied in manual labor, in other words, the more modern industry becomes developed, the more is the labor of men superseded by that of women. Differences of age and sex have no longer any distinctive social validity for the working class. All are instruments of labor, more or less expensive to use, according to their age and sex.

No sooner is the exploitation of the laborer by the manufacturer, so far at an end, that he receives his wages in cash, than he is set upon by the other portions of the bourgeoisie, the landlord, the shopkeeper, the pawnbroker, etc.

The ***lower strata of the middle class -- the small tradespeople, shopkeepers, retired tradesmen generally, the handicraftsmen and peasants -- all these sink gradually into the proletariat***, partly because their diminutive capital does not suffice for the scale on which Modern Industry is carried on, and is swamped in the competition with the large capitalists, partly because their specialized skill is rendered worthless by the new methods of production. Thus the ***proletariat is recruited from all classes of the population.***

The proletariat goes through various stages of development. With its birth begins its struggle with the bourgeoisie. At first the contest is carried on by individual laborers, then by the workpeople of a factory, then by the operatives of one trade, in one locality, against the individual bourgeois who directly exploits them. They direct their attacks not against the bourgeois conditions of production, but against the instruments of production themselves; they destroy imported wares that compete with their labor, they smash to pieces machinery, they set factories ablaze, they seek to restore by force the vanished status of the workman of the Middle Ages.

At this stage the *__laborers still form an incoherent mass scattered over the whole country,__* and broken up by their mutual competition. If anywhere they unite to form more compact bodies, this is not yet the consequence of their own active union, but of the union of the bourgeoisie, which class, in order to attain its own political ends, is compelled to set the whole proletariat in motion, and is moreover yet, for a time, able to do so. *__At this stage__*, therefore, the *__proletarians do not fight their enemies, but the enemies of their enemies,__* the remnants of absolute monarchy, the landowners, the non-industrial bourgeois, the petty bourgeoisie. Thus the whole historical movement is concentrated in the hands of the bourgeoisie; every victory so obtained is a victory for the bourgeoisie.

But *__with the development of industry the proletariat not only increases in number; it becomes concentrated in greater masses, its strength grows, and it feels that strength more.__* The various interests and conditions of life within the ranks of the proletariat are more and more equalized, in proportion as machinery obliterates all distinctions of labor, and nearly everywhere reduces wages to the same low level. The growing competition among the bourgeois, and the resulting commercial *__crises__*, make the wages of the workers ever more fluctuating. The unceasing improvement of machinery, ever more rapidly developing, makes their livelihood more and more precarious; the collisions between individual workmen and individual bourgeois take more and more the character of collisions between two classes. Thereupon the *__workers begin to form combinations (Trades__*

Unions [**Tool #1**]*) against the bourgeois;* they club together in order to keep up the rate of wages; they found permanent associations in order to make provision beforehand for these occasional revolts. Here and there the contest breaks out into riots.

Now and then the workers are victorious, but only for a time. The real fruit of their battles lies, not in the immediate result, but in the ever-expanding union of the workers. This union is helped on by the improved means of communication that are created by modern industry and that place the workers of different localities in contact with one another. It was just this contact that was needed to centralize the numerous local struggles, all of the same character, into one national struggle between classes. But every class struggle is a political struggle. And that union, to attain which the burghers of the Middle Ages, with their miserable highways, required centuries, the modern proletarians, thanks to railways, achieve in a few years.

This *organization of the proletarians into a class, and consequently into a political party* (**Strategy**), is continually being upset again by the competition between the workers themselves. But it ever rises up again, stronger, firmer, mightier. It *compels legislative recognition* of particular interests of the workers, by taking advantage of the divisions among the bourgeoisie itself. Thus the ten-hours' bill in England was carried.

Altogether collisions between the classes of the old society further, in many ways, the course of development of the proletariat. The bourgeoisie finds itself involved in a constant battle. At first with the aristocracy; later on, with those portions of the bourgeoisie itself, whose interests have become antagonistic to the progress of industry; at all times, with the bourgeoisie of foreign countries. In all these battles it sees itself compelled to appeal to the proletariat, to ask for its help, and thus, to drag it into the political arena. The bourgeoisie itself, therefore, supplies the proletariat with its own instruments of political and general education, in other words, it furnishes the proletariat with weapons for fighting the bourgeoisie.

Further, as we have already seen, entire sections of the ruling classes are, by the advance of industry, precipitated into the proletariat, or are at least threatened in their conditions of existence. These also supply the proletariat with fresh elements of enlightenment and progress.

Finally, in times when the class struggle nears the decisive hour, the process of dissolution going on within the ruling class, in fact within the whole range of society, assumes such a violent, glaring character, that a small section of the ruling class cuts itself adrift, and joins the revolutionary class, the class that holds the future in its hands. Just as, therefore, at an earlier period, a section of the nobility went over to the bourgeoisie, so now a portion of the bourgeoisie goes over to the proletariat, and in particular, a portion of the bourgeois ideologists, who have raised themselves to the level of comprehending theoretically the historical movement as a whole.

**Of all the classes that stand face to face with the bourgeoisie today, the proletariat alone is a really revolutionary class.** The other classes decay and finally disappear in the face of Modern Industry; the proletariat is its special and essential product. The _**lower middle class,**_ the small manufacturer, the shopkeeper, the artisan, the peasant, all these fight against the bourgeoisie, to save from extinction their existence as fractions of the middle class. They are therefore _**not revolutionary**_, but _**conservative**_. Nay more, they are _**reactionary**_, for they _**try to roll back the wheel of history.**_ If by chance they are revolutionary, they are so only in view of their impending transfer into the proletariat, they thus defend not their present, but their future interests, they desert their own standpoint to place themselves at that of the proletariat.

The _**"dangerous class," the social scum**_(non working poor), that passively rotting mass thrown off by the lowest layers of old society, may, here and there, be swept into the movement by a proletarian revolution; its conditions of life, however, prepare it far more for the part of a bribed tool of reactionary intrigue.

In the conditions of the proletariat, those of old society at large are already virtually swamped. The *proletarian is without property; his relation to his wife and children has no longer anything in common with the bourgeois family-relations;* modern industrial labor, modern subjection to capital, the same in England as in France, in America as in Germany, has *stripped him of every trace of national character. Law, morality, religion, are to him so many bourgeois prejudices,* behind which lurk in ambush just as many bourgeois interests.

All the preceding classes that got the upper hand, sought to fortify their already acquired status by subjecting society at large to their conditions of appropriation. The proletarians cannot become masters of the productive forces of society, except by abolishing their own previous mode of appropriation, and thereby also every other previous mode of appropriation. *They have nothing of their own to secure and to fortify; their mission is to destroy all previous securities for, and insurances of, individual property.*

All *previous historical movements* were *movements of minorities*, or in the interests of minorities. The *proletarian movement is the selfconscious, independent movement of the immense majority, in the interests of the immense majority. The proletariat, the lowest stratum of our present society, cannot stir, cannot raise itself up, without the whole superincumbent strata of official society being sprung into the air.*

Though not in substance, yet in form, the struggle of the proletariat with the bourgeoisie is *at first a national struggle.* The proletariat of each country must, of course, first of all settle matters with its own bourgeoisie.

In depicting the most general phases of the development of the proletariat, we traced the more or less veiled civil war, raging within existing society, up to the point where that war breaks out into open revolution, and where the *violent overthrow of the bourgeoisie lays the foundation for the sway of the proletariat.*

Hitherto, every form of society has been based, as we have

already seen, on the antagonism of oppressing and oppressed classes. But in order to oppress a class, certain conditions must be assured to it under which it can, at least, continue its slavish existence. The serf, in the period of serfdom, raised himself to membership in the commune, just as the petty bourgeois, under the yoke of feudal absolutism, managed to develop into a bourgeois. The ***modern laborer***, on the contrary, instead of rising with the progress of industry, sinks deeper and deeper below the conditions of existence of his own class. He ***becomes a pauper*** (**Critical Objective**), and pauperism develops more rapidly than population and wealth. And here it becomes evident, that the ***bourgeoisie is unfit any longer to be the ruling class in society***, and to impose its conditions of existence upon society as an over-riding law. ***It is unfit to rule because it is incompetent to assure an existence to its slave within his slavery, because it cannot help letting him sink into such a state, that it has to feed him, instead of being fed by him.*** Society can no longer live under this bourgeoisie, in other words, its existence is no longer compatible with society.

The ***essential condition for the existence, and for the sway of the bourgeois class, is the formation and augmentation of capital*** (**Destruction of Capital = Destruction of Bourgeoisie**); the condition for capital is wage-labor. Wage-labor rests exclusively on competition between the laborers. The advance of industry, whose involuntary promoter is the bourgeoisie, replaces the isolation of the laborers, due to competition, by their revolutionary combination, due to association. The development of Modern Industry, therefore, cuts from under its feet the very foundation on which the bourgeoisie produces and appropriates products. ***What the bourgeoisie, therefore, produces, above all, is its own grave-diggers. Its fall and the victory of the proletariat are equally inevitable.***

Section II. Proletarians and Communists

In **what relation do the Communists stand to the proletarians as a whole**?

The Communists do not form a separate party opposed to other working-class parties.

They have **no interests separate and apart from those of the proletariat** as a whole.

They do not set up any sectarian principles of their own, by which to shape and mould the proletarian movement.

The Communists are distinguished from the other working-class parties by this only:

1. In the national struggles of the proletarians of the different countries, they **point out and bring to the front the common interests of the entire proletariat, independently of all nationality.**

2. In the various stages of development which the struggle of the working class against the bourgeoisie has to pass through, **they always and everywhere represent the interests of the movement as a whole.**

The Communists, therefore, are on the one hand, practically, the **most advanced and resolute section of the working-class parties of every country,** that section which pushes forward all others; on the other hand, theoretically, they have over the great mass of the proletariat the **advantage of clearly understanding the line of march, the conditions, and the ultimate general results of the proletarian movement.**

The **immediate aim of the Communist** is the same as that of all the other proletarian parties: **formation of the proletariat into a class, overthrow of the bourgeois supremacy, conquest of political power by the proletariat.**

The theoretical conclusions of the Communists are in no way based on ideas or principles that have been invented, or discovered, by this or that would-be universal reformer. They merely express, in general terms, actual relations springing from an existing class struggle, from a historical movement going on under our very eyes. The abolition of existing property relations is not at all a distinctive feature of Communism.

All property relations in the past have continually been subject to historical change consequent upon the change in historical conditions.

The French Revolution, for example, abolished feudal property in favor of bourgeois property.

The distinguishing feature of Communism is not the abolition of property generally, but the ***abolition of bourgeois property***. But modern bourgeois private property is the final and most complete expression of the system of producing and appropriating products, that is based on class antagonisms, on the exploitation of the many by the few.

In this sense, ***the theory of the Communists*** may be ***summed up*** in the single sentence: ***Abolition of private property.*** (**Desired End Result**)

We Communists have been reproached with the desire of abolishing the right of personally acquiring property as the fruit of a man's own labor, which property is alleged to be the groundwork of all personal freedom, activity and independence.

Hard-won, self-acquired, self-earned property! Do you mean the property of the petty artisan and of the small peasant, a form of property that preceded the bourgeois form? There is no need to abolish that; the development of industry has to a great extent already destroyed it, and is still destroying it daily.

Or do you mean modern bourgeois private property?

But ***does wage-labor create any property for the laborer? Not a bit. It creates capital,*** i.e., that kind of property which exploits wage-labor, and which cannot increase except upon condition of begetting a new supply of wage-labor for fresh exploitation. Property, in its present form, is based on the antagonism of capital and wage-labor. Let us examine both sides of this antagonism.

To be a capitalist, is to have not only a purely personal, but a social status in production. Capital is a collective product, and only by the united action of many members, nay, in the last resort, only by the united action of all members of society, can it be set in motion.

Capital is, therefore, not a personal, it is *a social power.*

When, therefore, *capital is converted into common property, into the property of all members of society, personal property is not* thereby transformed into social property. It is only the social character of the property that is changed. It loses its class-character.

Let us now take wage-labor.

The *average price of wage-labor is the minimum wage*, i.e., that quantum of the means of subsistence, which is absolutely requisite in bare existence as a laborer. What, therefore, the wage-laborer appropriates by means of his labor, merely suffices to prolong and reproduce a bare existence. *We by no means intend to abolish this personal appropriation of the products of labor, an appropriation that is made for the maintenance and reproduction of human life,* and that leaves no surplus wherewith to command the labor of others. All that *we want to do away with, is the miserable character of this appropriation,* under which the laborer lives merely to increase capital, and is allowed to live only in so far as the interest of the ruling class requires it.

In bourgeois society, living labor is but a means to increase accumulated labor. In Communist society, accumulated labor is but a means to widen, to enrich, to promote the existence of the laborer.

In *bourgeois society,* therefore, the *past dominates the present;* in *Communist society,* the *present dominates the past* (**a critically important concept when planning educational curriculum. In the 1970's, U.S. public schools replaced history and like courses with Social Studies [AKA Socialism], resulting in "historically illiterate" students and graduates**). In bourgeois society capital is independent and has individuality, while the living person is dependent and has no individuality.

And the abolition of this state of things is called by the bourgeois, abolition of individuality and freedom! And rightly so. The ***abolition of bourgeois individuality, bourgeois independence, and bourgeois freedom is undoubtedly aimed at.***

By freedom is meant, under the present bourgeois conditions of production, free trade, free selling and buying.

But if selling and buying disappears, free selling and buying disappears also. This talk about free selling and buying, and all the other "brave words" of our bourgeoisie about freedom in general, have a meaning, if any, only in contrast with restricted selling and buying, with the fettered traders of the Middle Ages, but have no meaning when opposed to the Communistic abolition of buying and selling, of the bourgeois conditions of production, and of the bourgeoisie itself.

You are horrified at our intending to do away with private property. But in your existing society, private property is already done away with for nine-tenths of the population; its existence for the few is solely due to its non-existence in the hands of those nine-tenths. You reproach us, therefore, with intending to do away with a form of property, the necessary condition for whose existence is the non-existence of any property for the immense majority of society.

In one word, you reproach us with intending to do away with your property. Precisely so; that is just what we intend.

From the moment when labor can no longer be converted into capital, money, or rent, into a social power capable of being monopolized, i.e., from the moment when individual property can no longer be transformed into bourgeois property, into capital, from that moment, you say individuality vanishes.

You must, therefore, confess that by ***"individual"*** you mean no other person than the bourgeois, than ***the middle-class owner of property. This person must, indeed, be swept out of the way, and*** _**made impossible.**_

**Communism deprives no man of the power to appropriate the products of society; all that it does is to deprive him of the power to subjugate the labor of others by means of such appropriation.**

It has been objected that upon the abolition of private property all work will cease, and universal laziness will overtake us.

According to this, _**bourgeois society ought long ago to have gone to the dogs through sheer idleness;**_ for those of its members who work, acquire nothing, and _**those who acquire anything, do not work.**_ The whole of this objection is but another expression of the tautology: that there can no longer be any wage-labor when there is no longer any capital.

All objections urged against the Communistic mode of producing and appropriating material products, have, in the same way, been urged against the Communistic modes of producing and appropriating intellectual products. Just as, to the bourgeois, the disappearance of class property is the disappearance of production itself, so the disappearance of class culture is to him identical with the disappearance of all culture.

That _**culture**_, the loss of which he laments, is, for the enormous majority, a _**mere training to act as a machine.**_

But don't wrangle with us so long as you apply, to our intended abolition of bourgeois property, the standard of your bourgeois notions of freedom, culture, law, etc. Your very ideas are but the outgrowth of the conditions of your bourgeois production and bourgeois property, just as your jurisprudence is but the will of your class made into a law for all, a will, whose essential character and direction are determined by the economical conditions of existence of your class.

The selfish misconception that induces you to transform into eternal laws of nature and of reason, the social forms springing from your present mode of production and form of property -- historical relations that rise and disappear in the progress of production -- this misconception you share with every ruling class that has preceded you. What you see clearly in the case of ancient property, what you admit in the case of feudal property, you are of course forbidden to admit in the case of your own bourgeois form of property.

Abolition of the family! Even the most radical flare up at this infamous proposal of the Communists.

On what foundation is the present family, the bourgeois family, based? On capital, on private gain. In its completely developed form this family exists only among the bourgeoisie. But this state of things finds its complement in the practical absence of the family among the proletarians, and in public prostitution (**since 1960's, state and federal laws passed that facilitated divorce [AKA no fault divorce] and supported single parenthood**).

The bourgeois family will vanish as a matter of course when its complement vanishes, and both will vanish with the vanishing of capital.

Do you charge us with wanting to ***stop the exploitation of children by their parents***? To this crime we plead guilty.

But, you will say, we destroy the most hallowed of relations, when we ***replace home education by social.***

And your education! Is not that also social, and determined by the social conditions under which you educate, by the intervention, direct or indirect, of society, by means of schools, etc.? The ***Communists*** have not invented the intervention of society in education; they do but seek to alter the character of that intervention, and to ***rescue education from the influence of the ruling class.*** (**In 1935, Columbia University in New York City welcomed dissident Marxist scholars from the "Frankfurt School" into their faculty. They were fleeing the University of Frankfurt because of Hitler's rise in power and the growing influence in Germany of "National" Socialism. The ramifications of their teachings now extend to all of U.S. academia**).

The bourgeois clap-trap about the family and education, about the hallowed co-relation of parent and child, becomes all the more disgusting, the more, by the action of Modern Industry, ***all family ties among the proletarians are torn asunder***, and their children transformed into simple articles of commerce and instruments of labor.

But you Communists would introduce community of women, screams the whole bourgeoisie in chorus.

The bourgeois sees in his wife a mere instrument of production. He hears that the instruments of production are to be exploited in common, and, naturally, can come to no other conclusion than that the lot of being common to all will likewise fall to the women.

He has not even a suspicion that the ***real point is to do away with the status of women as mere instruments of production*** (in 1973 the US Supreme Court decision on Roe v. Wade incorporated recommendations for easy access to abortion, subsequently the use of abortion for birth control and the push for premarital sex [AKA sexual revolution] rose).

For the rest, nothing is more ridiculous than the virtuous indignation of our bourgeois at the community of women which, they pretend, is to be openly and officially established by the Communists. The Communists have no need to introduce community of women; it has existed almost from time immemorial.

Our bourgeois, not content with having the wives and daughters of their proletarians at their disposal, not to speak of common prostitutes, take the greatest pleasure in seducing each other's wives.

Bourgeois marriage is in reality a system of wives in common and thus, at the most, what the Communists might possibly be reproached with, is that they desire to introduce, in substitution for a hypocritically concealed, an openly legalized community of women. For the rest, it is self-evident that the abolition of the present system of production must bring with it the abolition of the community of women springing from that system, i.e., of prostitution both public and private.

The ***Communists are further reproached with desiring to abolish countries and nationality.***

No Country = No Nation = No Borders

The ***working men have no country.*** We cannot take from them what they have not got. Since the ***proletariat must first of all acquire political supremacy,*** must rise to be the leading class of the nation, must constitute itself the nation, it is, so far, itself national, though not in the bourgeois sense of the word.

National differences and antagonisms between peoples are daily more and more vanishing, owing to the development of the bourgeoisie, to freedom of commerce, to the world-market, to uniformity in the mode of production and in the conditions of life corresponding thereto.

The supremacy of the proletariat will cause them to vanish still faster. *United action, of the leading civilized countries at least, is one of the first conditions for the emancipation of the proletariat.* **(United Nations, 1992, Agenda 21)**

In proportion as the exploitation of one individual by another is put an end to, the exploitation of one nation by another will also be put an end to. In proportion as the antagonism between classes within the nation vanishes, the hostility of one nation to another will come to an end.

The *charges against Communism made from a religious, a philosophical, and, generally, from an ideological standpoint, are not deserving of serious examination.*

Does it require deep intuition to comprehend that man's ideas, views and conceptions, in one word, man's consciousness, changes with every change in the conditions of his material existence, in his social relations and in his social life?

What else does the history of ideas prove, than that intellectual production changes its character in proportion as material production is changed? The ruling ideas of each age have ever been the ideas of its ruling class.

When people speak of ideas that revolutionize society, they do but express the fact, that within the old society, the elements of a new one have been created, and that the dissolution of the old ideas keeps even pace with the dissolution of the old conditions of existence.

When the ancient world was in its last throes, *the ancient religions were overcome by Christianity.* **(Instead of "overcoming,"**

Christians failed to recover and keep Jerusalem/the Holy Land from the Moslems with their Crusades, seven or more military expeditions from the 11th to the end of the 13th century, and barely managed to keep the Moslems [also known as Muslims and Islamists] from overrunning and occupying Europe). When Christian ideas succumbed in the 18th century to rationalist ideas, feudal society fought its death battle with the then revolutionary bourgeoisie. The ideas of religious liberty and freedom of conscience merely gave expression to the sway of free competition within the domain of knowledge.

"Undoubtedly," it will be said, "religious, moral, philosophical, and juridical ideas have been modified in the course of historical development. But religion, morality, philosophy, political science, and law constantly survived this change."

"There are, besides, eternal truths, such as Freedom, Justice, etc. that are common to all states of society. ___But Communism abolishes eternal truths, it abolishes all religion, and all morality,___ (Critically important -- most Communists are atheists),** instead of constituting them on a new basis; it therefore acts in contradiction to all past historical experience."

What does this accusation reduce itself to? The ___history___ of all past society has consisted in the development of ___class antagonisms___, antagonisms that assumed different forms at different epochs.

But whatever form they may have taken, one fact is common to all past ages, viz., the ___exploitation of one part of society by the other___. No wonder, then, that the social consciousness of past ages, despite all the multiplicity and variety it displays, moves within certain common forms, or general ideas, which cannot completely vanish except with the total disappearance of class antagonisms.

The Communist revolution is the most radical rupture with traditional property relations; no wonder that its development involves the most radical rupture with traditional ideas.

But let us have done with the bourgeois objections to Communism.

We have seen above, that the *__first step in the revolution by the working class, is to raise the proletariat to the position of ruling as to win the battle of democracy.__*

The *__proletariat will use its political supremacy to wrest, by degrees, all capital from the bourgeoisie, to centralize all instruments of production in the hands of the State, i.e., of the proletariat organized as the ruling class; and to increase the total of productive forces as rapidly as possible.__* (**Critically important**)

Of course, in the beginning, this cannot be effected except by means of despotic inroads on the rights of property, and on the conditions of bourgeois production; by means of measures, therefore, which appear economically insufficient and untenable, but which, in the course of the movement, outstrip themselves, necessitate further inroads upon the old social order, and are unavoidable as a means of entirely *__revolutionizing__* the mode of production.

These measures will of course be different in different countries.

Nevertheless *__in the most advanced countries, the following will be pretty generally applicable.__*

1. Abolition of property in land and application of all rents of land to public purposes. (**the Supreme Court decided in 2005, Kelo v. City of New London, 545 U.S. 469, that eminent domain power, that is the government seizure of and payment for private land without the consent of the owner, could be used not only for public purposes like roads and schools but also to increase municipal revenues**)

2. A heavy progressive or graduated income tax. (**16th Amendment to the Constitution of the United States, added in 1913, a confiscatory [not a consumption] tax**)

3. Abolition of all right of inheritance.

4. Confiscation of the property of all emigrants and rebels.

5. Centralization of credit in the hands of the State, by means of a national bank with State capital and an exclusive monopoly.

6. Centralization of the means of communication and transport

in the hands of the State.

7. Extension of factories and instruments of production owned by the State; the bringing into cultivation of waste-lands, and the improvement of the soil generally in accordance with a common plan.

8. Equal liability of all to labor. Establishment of industrial armies, especially for agriculture.

9. Combination of agriculture with manufacturing industries; gradual abolition of the distinction between town and country, by a more equable distribution of the population over the country.

10. Free education for all children in public schools. Abolition of children's factory labor in its present form. Combination of education with industrial production, &c., &c. (**For indoctrination or dumbing down**)

When, in the course of development, class distinctions have disappeared, and ***all production has been concentrated in the hands of a vast association of the whole nation, the public power will lose its political character***. Political power, properly so called, is merely the ***organized power of one class for oppressing another.*** If the proletariat during its contest with the bourgeoisie is compelled, by the force of circumstances, to organize itself as a class, if, by means of a revolution, it makes itself the ruling class, and, as such, sweeps away by force the old conditions of production, then it will, along with these conditions, have swept away the conditions for the existence of class antagonisms and of classes generally, and will thereby have abolished its own supremacy as a class.

In place of the old bourgeois society, with its classes and class antagonisms, we shall have ***an association,*** in which the ***free development of each is the condition for the free development of all.***

(**But NO incentive for the individual**)

Section III. Socialist and Communist Literature

1. REACTIONARY SOCIALISM

A. Feudal Socialism

Owing to their historical position, it became the vocation of the aristocracies of France and England to write pamphlets against modern bourgeois society. In the French revolution of July 1830, and in the English reform agitation, these aristocracies again succumbed to the hateful upstart. Thenceforth, a serious political contest was altogether out of the question. A literary battle alone remained possible. But even in the domain of literature the old cries of the restoration period had become impossible.

In order to arouse sympathy, the aristocracy were obliged to lose sight, apparently, of their own interests, and to formulate their indictment against the bourgeoisie in the interest of the exploited working class alone. Thus the aristocracy took their revenge by singing lampoons on their new master, and whispering in his ears sinister prophecies of coming catastrophe.

In this way arose ***Feudal Socialism***: half lamentation, half lampoon; half echo of the past, half menace of the future; at times, by its bitter, witty and incisive criticism, striking the bourgeoisie to the very heart's core; but ***always ludicrous*** in its effect, through total incapacity to comprehend the march of modern history.

The aristocracy, in order to rally the people to them, waved the proletarian alms-bag in front for a banner. But the people, so often as it joined them, saw on their hindquarters the old feudal coats of arms, and deserted with loud and irreverent laughter.

One section of the French Legitimists and "Young England" exhibited this spectacle.

In pointing out that their mode of exploitation was different to that of the bourgeoisie, the feudalists forget that they exploited under circumstances and conditions that were quite different, and that are now antiquated. In showing that, under their rule, the modern proletariat never existed, they forget that the modern bourgeoisie is the necessary offspring of their own form of society.

For the rest, so little do they conceal the reactionary character of their criticism that their chief accusation against the bourgeoisie amounts to this, that under the bourgeois regime a class is being developed, which is destined to cut up root and branch the old order of society.

What they upbraid the bourgeoisie with is not so much that it creates a proletariat, as that it creates a revolutionary proletariat.

In political practice, therefore, they join in all coercive measures against the working class; and in ordinary life, despite their high falutin phrases, they stoop to pick up the golden apples dropped from the tree of industry, and to barter truth, love, and honor for traffic in wool, beetrootsugar, and potato spirits.

As the parson has ever gone band in hand with the landlord, so has Clerical Socialism with Feudal Socialism.

Nothing is easier than to give Christian asceticism a Socialist tinge. Has not Christianity declaimed against private property, against marriage, against the State? Has it not preached in the place of these, charity and poverty, celibacy and mortification of the flesh, monastic life and Mother Church? Christian Socialism is but the holy water with which the priest consecrates the heart-burnings of the aristocrat.

B. Petty-Bourgeois Socialism

The feudal aristocracy was not the only class that was ruined by the bourgeoisie, not the only class whose conditions of existence pined and perished in the atmosphere of modern bourgeois society. The mediaeval burgesses and the small peasant proprietors were the precursors of the modern bourgeoisie. In those countries which are but little developed, industrially and commercially, these two classes still vegetate side by side with the rising bourgeoisie.

In countries where modern civilization has become fully developed, a new class of petty bourgeois has been formed, fluctuating between proletariat and bourgeoisie and ever renewing itself as a supplementary part of bourgeois society. The individual members of this class, however, are being constantly hurled down into the proletariat by the action of competition, and, as modern industry develops, they even see the moment approaching when they will completely disappear as an independent section of modern society, to be replaced, in manufactures, agriculture and commerce, by overlookers, bailiffs and shopmen.

In countries like France, where the peasants constitute far more than half of the population, it was natural that writers who sided with the proletariat against the bourgeoisie, should use, in their criticism of the bourgeois regime, the standard of the peasant and petty bourgeois, and from the standpoint of these intermediate classes should take up the cudgels for the working class. Thus arose petty-bourgeois Socialism. Sismondi was the head of this school, not only in France but also in England.

This school of Socialism dissected with great acuteness the contradictions in the conditions of modern production. It laid bare the hypocritical apologies of economists. It proved, incontrovertibly, the disastrous effects of machinery and division of labor; the concentration of capital and land in a few hands; overproduction and **_crises_**; it pointed out the inevitable ruin of the petty bourgeois and peasant, the misery of the proletariat, the anarchy in production, the crying inequalities in the distribution of wealth, the industrial war of extermination between nations, the dissolution of old moral bonds, of the old family relations, of the old nationalities.

In its positive aims, however, this form of Socialism aspires either to restoring the old means of production and of exchange, and with them the old property relations, and the old society, or to cramping the modern means of production and of exchange, within the framework of the old property relations that have been, and were bound to be, exploded by those means. In either case, it is both ***reactionary and Utopian***.

Its last words are: corporate guilds for manufacture, patriarchal relations in agriculture.

Ultimately, when stubborn historical facts had dispersed all intoxicating effects of self-deception, ***this form of Socialism ended in a miserable fit of the blues***.

C. German, or "True," Socialism (Root of Nazism)

The Socialist and Communist literature of France, a literature that originated under the pressure of a bourgeoisie in power, and that was the expression of the struggle against this power, was introduced into Germany at a time when the bourgeoisie, in that country, had just begun its contest with feudal absolutism.

German philosophers, would-be philosophers, and beaux esprits, eagerly seized on this literature, only forgetting, that when these writings immigrated from France into Germany, French social conditions had not immigrated along with them. In contact with German social conditions, this French literature lost all its immediate practical significance, and assumed a purely literary aspect. Thus, to the German philosophers of the eighteenth century, the demands of the first French Revolution were nothing more than the demands of "Practical Reason" in general, and the utterance of the will of the revolutionary French bourgeoisie signified in their eyes the law of pure Will, of Will as it was bound to be, of true human Will generally.

The world of the German literate consisted solely in bringing the new French ideas into harmony with their ancient philosophical conscience, or rather, in annexing the French ideas without deserting their own philosophic point of view.

This annexation took place in the same way in which a foreign language is appropriated, namely, by translation.

It is well known how the monks wrote silly lives of Catholic Saints over the manuscripts on which the classical works of ancient heathendom had been written. The German literate reversed this process with the profane French literature. They wrote their philosophical nonsense beneath the French original. For instance, beneath the French criticism of the economic functions of money, they wrote "Alienation of Humanity," and beneath the French criticism of the bourgeois State they wrote "dethronement of the Category of the General," and so forth.

The introduction of these philosophical phrases at the back of the French historical criticisms they dubbed "Philosophy of Action," "True Socialism," "German Science of Socialism," "Philosophical Foundation of Socialism," and so on.

The French Socialist and Communist literature was thus completely emasculated. And, since it ceased in the hands of the German to express the struggle of one class with the other, he felt conscious of having overcome "French one-sidedness" and of representing, not true requirements, but the requirements of truth; not the interests of the proletariat, but the interests of Human Nature, of Man in general, who belongs to no class, has no reality, who exists only in the misty realm of philosophical fantasy.

This German Socialism, which took its schoolboy task so seriously and solemnly, and extolled its poor stock-in-trade in such mountebank fashion, meanwhile gradually lost its pedantic innocence.

The fight of the German, and especially, of the Prussian bourgeoisie, against feudal aristocracy and absolute monarchy, in other words, the ***liberal movement***, became more earnest.

By this, the long wished-for opportunity was offered to "True" Socialism of confronting the political movement with the Socialist demands, of hurling the traditional anathemas against liberalism, against representative government, against bourgeois competition, bourgeois freedom of the press, bourgeois legislation, bourgeois liberty and equality, and of preaching to the masses that they had nothing to gain, and everything to lose, by this bourgeois movement. ***German***

__Socialism forgot, in the nick of time, that the French criticism, whose silly echo it was, presupposed the existence of modern bourgeois society, with its corresponding economic conditions of existence, and the political constitution adapted thereto, the very things whose attainment was the object of the pending struggle in Germany.__

To the absolute governments, with their following of parsons, professors, country squires and officials, it served as a welcome scarecrow against the threatening bourgeoisie.

It was a sweet finish after the bitter pills of floggings and bullets with which these same governments, just at that time, dosed the German working-class risings.

While this "True" Socialism thus served the governments as a weapon for fighting the German bourgeoisie, it, at the same time, directly represented a reactionary interest, the interest of the German Philistines. In Germany the petty-bourgeois class, a relic of the sixteenth century, and since then constantly cropping up again under various forms, is the real social basis of the existing state of things.

To preserve this class is to preserve the existing state of things in Germany. The industrial and political supremacy of the bourgeoisie threatens it with certain destruction; on the one hand, from the concentration of capital; on the other, from the rise of a revolutionary proletariat. "True" Socialism appeared to kill these two birds with one stone. It spread like an epidemic.

The robe of speculative cobwebs, embroidered with flowers of rhetoric, steeped in the dew of sickly sentiment, this transcendental robe in which the German Socialists wrapped their sorry "eternal truths," all skin and bone, served to wonderfully increase the sale of their goods amongst such a public. And on its part, German Socialism recognized, more and more, its own calling as the bombastic representative of the petty- bourgeois Philistine.

It proclaimed the German nation to be the model nation (**racist component of Nazism**), and the German petty Philistine to be the typical man. To every villainous meanness of this model man it gave a hidden, higher, Socialistic interpretation, the exact contrary of its real character. ***It went to the extreme length of directly opposing the "brutally destructive" tendency of Communism***, and of proclaiming its supreme and impartial contempt of all class struggles. With very few exceptions, all the so-called Socialist and Communist publications that now (1847) circulate in Germany belong to the domain of this foul and enervating literature.

2. CONSERVATIVE, OR BOURGEOIS, SOCIALISM

A part of the bourgeoisie is desirous of redressing social grievances, in order to secure the continued existence of bourgeois society.

To this section belong ***economists, philanthropists, humanitarians, improvers of the condition of the working class, organizers of charity, members of societies for the prevention of cruelty to animals, temperance fanatics, hole-and-corner reformers of every imaginable kind.*** This form of Socialism has, moreover, been worked out into complete systems.

We may cite Proudhon's Philosophie de la Misere as an example of this form.

The Socialistic bourgeois want all the advantages of modern social conditions without the struggles and dangers necessarily resulting therefrom. They desire the existing state of society minus its revolutionary and disintegrating elements. They wish for a bourgeoisie without a proletariat. The bourgeoisie naturally conceives the world in which it is supreme to be the best; and bourgeois Socialism develops this comfortable conception into various more or less complete systems. In requiring the proletariat to carry out such a system, and thereby to march straightway into the social New Jerusalem, it but requires in reality, that the proletariat should remain within the bounds of existing society, but should cast away all its hateful ideas concerning the bourgeoisie.

A second and more practical, but less systematic, form of this

Socialism sought to depreciate every revolutionary movement in the eyes of the working class, by showing that no mere political reform, but only a change in the material conditions of existence, in economic relations, could be of any advantage to them. By changes in the material conditions of existence, this form of Socialism, however, by no means understands abolition of the bourgeois relations of production, an abolition that can be effected only by a revolution, but administrative reforms, based on the continued existence of these relations; reforms, therefore, that in no respect affect the relations between capital and labor, but, at the best, lessen the cost, and simplify the administrative work, of bourgeois government.

Bourgeois Socialism attains adequate expression, when, and only when, it becomes a mere figure of speech.

Free trade: for the benefit of the working class. Protective duties: for the benefit of the working class. Prison Reform: for the benefit of the working class. This is the last word and the only seriously meant word of bourgeois Socialism.

It is summed up in the phrase: the ***bourgeois is a bourgeois -- for the benefit of the working class.***

3. CRITICAL-UTOPIAN SOCIALISM AND COMMUNISM

We do not here refer to that literature which, in every great modern revolution, has always given voice to the demands of the proletariat, such as the writings of Babeuf and others.

The first direct attempts of the proletariat to attain its own ends, made in times of universal excitement, when feudal society was being overthrown, these attempts necessarily failed, owing to the then undeveloped state of the proletariat, as well as to the absence of the economic conditions for its emancipation, conditions that had yet to be produced, and could be produced by the impending bourgeois epoch alone. The revolutionary literature that accompanied these first movements of the proletariat had necessarily a reactionary character. It inculcated universal asceticism and social leveling in its crudest form.

The Socialist and Communist systems properly so called, those of Saint-Simon, Fourier, Owen and others, spring into existence in the early undeveloped period, described above, of the struggle between proletariat and bourgeoisie (see Section 1. Bourgeois and Proletarians).

The founders of these systems see, indeed, the class antagonisms, as well as the action of the decomposing elements, in the prevailing form of society. But the ***proletariat, as yet in its infancy, offers to them the spectacle of a class without any historical initiative or any independent political movement.***

Since the development of class antagonism keeps even pace with the development of industry, the economic situation, as they find it, does not as yet offer to them the material conditions for the emancipation of the proletariat. They therefore search after a new social science, after new social laws, that are to create these conditions.

Historical action is to yield to their personal inventive action, historically created conditions of emancipation to fantastic ones, and the gradual, spontaneous class-organization of the proletariat to the organization of society specially contrived by these inventors. Future history resolves itself, in their eyes, into the propaganda and the practical carrying out of their social plans.

In the formation of their plans they are conscious of caring chiefly for the interests of the working class, as being the most suffering class. ***Only from the point of view of being the most suffering class does the proletariat exist for them.***

The undeveloped state of the class struggle, as well as their own surroundings, causes Socialists of this kind to consider themselves far superior to all class antagonisms. They want to improve the condition of every member of society, even that of the most favored. Hence, they habitually appeal to society at large, without distinction of class; nay, by preference, to the ruling class. For how can people, when once they understand their system, fail to see in it the best possible plan of the best possible state of society?

Hence, they reject all political, and especially all revolutionary, action; they wish to attain their ends by peaceful means, and endeavor, by small experiments, necessarily doomed to failure, and by the force of example, to pave the way for the new social Gospel.

Such fantastic pictures of future society, painted at a time when the proletariat is still in a very undeveloped state and has but a fantastic conception of its own position correspond with the first instinctive yearnings of that class for a general reconstruction of society.

But these Socialist and Communist publications contain also a critical element. They attack every principle of existing society. Hence they are full of the most valuable materials for the enlightenment of the working class. The practical measures proposed in them -- such as the abolition of the distinction between town and country, of the family, of the carrying on of industries for the account of private individuals, and of the wage system, the proclamation of social harmony, the conversion of the functions of the State into a mere superintendence of production, all these proposals, point solely to the disappearance of class antagonisms which were, at that time, only just cropping up, and which, in these publications, are recognized in their earliest, indistinct and undefined forms only. These ***proposals***, therefore, ***are of a purely Utopian character.***

The significance of Critical-Utopian Socialism and Communism bears an inverse relation to historical development. In proportion as the modern class struggle develops and takes definite shape, this fantastic standing apart from the contest, these fantastic attacks on it, lose all practical value and all theoretical justification. Therefore, although the ***originators of these systems were, in many respects, revolutionary, their disciples have, in every case, formed mere reactionary sects***. They hold fast by the original views of their masters, in opposition to the ***progressive*** historical development of the proletariat. They, therefore, ***endeavor***, and that consistently, ***to deaden the class struggle and to reconcile the class antagonisms.***

They still dream of experimental realization of their social Utopias, of founding isolated "phalansteres," of establishing "Home Colonies," of setting up a "Little Icaria" -- duodecimo editions of the New Jerusalem -- and to realize all these castles in the air, they are compelled to appeal to the feelings and purses of the bourgeois. ***By degrees they sink into the category of the reactionary conservative Socialists depicted above***, differing from these only by more systematic pedantry, and by their fanatical and superstitious belief in the miraculous effects of their social science.

They, therefore, violently oppose all political action on the part of the working class; such action, according to them, can only result from blind unbelief in the new Gospel.

The Owenites in England, and the Fourierists in France, respectively, oppose the Chartists and the Reformists.

Major Tools and/or Agents for Communists:

#1 Trade Unions
#2 Socialists

Section IV. Position of the Communists in Relation to the Various Existing Opposition Parties

Section II has made clear the relations of the Communists to the existing working-class parties, such as the Chartists in England and the Agrarian Reformers in America.

The Communists fight for the attainment of the immediate aims, for the enforcement of the momentary interests of the working class; but in the movement of the present, they also represent and take care of the future of that movement. In France the Communists ally themselves with the Social-Democrats, against the conservative and radical bourgeoisie, reserving, however, the right to take up a critical position in regard to phrases and illusions traditionally handed down from the great Revolution.

In Switzerland they support the Radicals, without losing sight of the fact that this party consists of antagonistic elements, partly of Democratic Socialists, in the French sense, partly of radical bourgeois.

In Poland they support the party that insists on an agrarian revolution as the prime condition for national emancipation, that party which fomented the insurrection of Cracow in 1846.

In Germany they fight with the bourgeoisie whenever it acts in a revolutionary way, against the absolute monarchy, the feudal squirearchy, and the petty bourgeoisie.

But they never cease, for a single instant, to instill into the working class the clearest possible recognition of the hostile antagonism between bourgeoisie and proletariat, in order that the German workers may straightaway use, as so many weapons against the bourgeoisie, the social and political conditions that the bourgeoisie must necessarily introduce along with its supremacy, and in order that, after the fall of the reactionary classes in Germany, the fight against the bourgeoisie itself may immediately begin.

The Communists turn their attention chiefly to Germany,

because that country is on the eve of a bourgeois revolution that is bound to be carried out under more advanced conditions of European civilization, and with a much more developed proletariat, than that of England was in the seventeenth, and of France in the eighteenth century, and because the bourgeois revolution in Germany will be but the prelude to an immediately following proletarian revolution.

In short, the Communists everywhere support every revolutionary movement against the existing social and political order of things. (layman's definition of a Communist: A Socialist with a gun [original source unknown])

In all these movements they bring to the front, as the leading question in each, *the property question,* no matter what its degree of development at the time.

Finally, *they labor everywhere for the union and agreement of the democratic parties of all countries.* "democratic parties"

The Communists disdain to conceal their views and aims. They openly declare that their ends can be attained only by the forcible overthrow of all existing social conditions. Let the ruling classes tremble at a Communistic revolution. The proletarians have nothing to lose but their chains. They have a world to win.

WORKING MEN OF ALL COUNTRIES, UNITE! (The End)

Agenda 21/Sustainable Development

AKA The Communist Manifesto of 1992

In June of 1992, the United Nations (U.N.) produced an "Agenda 21" for "sustainable development" at the U.N. Conference on Environment & Development in Rio De Janerio, Brazil. President George H. W. Bush (Republican) signed it, along with 178 countries, as a legally nonbinding statement of intent and not a treaty requiring ratification by the United States Senate. Representative Nancy Pelosi, Senator John Kerry, and Senator Harry Reid (Democrats) spoke in Congress in support of it. President Bill Clinton (Democrat) signed the first executive order to implement the "soft law" (U.N. Agenda 21: Environmental Piracy, Paugh).

Agenda 21 (21 for 21st Century) depicts the environmentalists' version of the Marxist "utopia" of communism. It describes sharing the wealth with developing countries at the expense and loss of the middle class in developed countries. Its implementation is to result in a global society with a central government that dictates where everyone lives, what they eat, when they move, as well as what resources or energy sources they may use. The agenda's comprehensive plan of action is to result in global government by a small elite group. Since the plan is consistent with the Communist Manifesto of 1848, I refer to it as the Communist Manifesto of 1992.

According to the Freedom Advocates online white paper and pamphlet, last revised in 2010, "Understanding Sustainable Development — Agenda 21: For the People and their Public Officials," the United Nations accredited more than 2000 Non-Governmental Organizations (NGOs) to implement Agenda 21 in America, for which the U.S. government gives them massive tax advantages. The list of NGOs includes the Nature Conservancy, the Sierra Club, the National Audubon Society, the American Planning

Association, the National Teachers Association, the U.S. Chamber of Commerce, and the U.S. Farm Bureau. The map titled "Simulated Reserve and Corridor System to Protect Diversity" shows how the U.S. will be 50% uninhabited after rural control through the Wildlands Network (AKA Wildlands Project) and urban control through Smart Growth (AKA "comprehensive planning" or "growth management") are in place. A major component to the creation of the desired North American Union (NAU), with political-economic equalization of Mexico, Canada, and the United States, is the development of the Trans-Texas Corridor by multi-national corporations in "public/private partnership" with government/s. More information at *freedomadvocates.org* and the American Policy Center at *americanpolicy.org.*

Excerpt from Blog www.dianesvann.com Aug 27, 2023 Earth produces oil and gas like the human body produces urine, feces, and gas. . . While the human body expels its waste products through its urinary and gastrointestinal tracts, the earth expels them through its volcanoes. The emptying of underground spaces result in earthquakes. Since man has been smartly digging up these products and using them for fuel, the earth has relaxed its reliance on volcanoes and earthquakes. . . United Nations produced Agenda 21. . . makes the earth's excrement untouchable. So that means the inevitable return of volcanoes and earthquakes on a large scale. . . . For an outstanding and rather recent (1816) example of a volcano's possible impact on both climate and the environment, read about the eruption of Mount Tambora on 10 April 1815 starting the Year Without a Summer.

For link to Wikipedia's description go to WEBSITE REFERENCE LIST #51 (WRL 51) on Page 151. Watch 5 minute videos "What's wrong with Wind and Solar?" and "A World without Fossil Fuels" (WRL 52).

President Obama's Communist Agenda

Yes Folks, we had a Communist in the White House. (If not, why did he, his community of czars, and the other Democratic Party leaders including Senate Majority Leader Harry Reid and House Minority Leader Nancy Pelosi demonstrably follow the Communist Manifesto?)

Karl Marx, after assessing all of the parties of the day in 1848, selected the Democratic Party to advance the Communist agenda. Obama was the perfect President of the United States for Marx's Democratic party. Communism was so ingrained in him from childhood.

On these pages I list President Obama's communist agenda, some of his presidential actions to achieve it, and pertinent explanatory and/or supportive text in the <u>Communist Manifesto</u>.

President Obama (and his czars):

1. Communist agenda: Continue the dumbing down of public education

Produce controllable followers who will not resist the new world order.

Obama's actions

1. *cut off funding for the DC Opportunity Scholarship Program in May 2009, a popular voucher program for students in Washington, DC to escape failing public schools.*
2. *did not renew a $170 million 2-year program to fund Historically*

Black Colleges and Universities in 2009. Accused of neglecting historically Black colleges in October 9, 2013 article by Brandon Brice in Washington Times online.

3. *In 2009 Obama took over student college loans from banks. Following explanation quoted from September 12, 2009 article "The Quietist Trillion: Congratulations. You're about to own $100 billion a year in student loans" in the Wall Street Journal online:*

The Obama plan calls for the U.S. Department of Education to move from its current 20% share of the student-loan origination market to 80% on July 1, 2010, when private lenders will be barred from making government-guaranteed loans. The remaining 20% of the market that is now completely private will likely shrink further as lenders try to comply with regulations Congress created last year. Starting next summer, taxpayers will have to put up roughly $100 billion per year to lend to students.

***

For decades, loans carrying a federal guarantee have been the most common way of borrowing for college. After raising money in the private capital markets, lenders made the loans, paying a fee to the government for each one. The government covered most of the cost of defaults while allowing the private lenders to make a regulated return.

The system broke down after Congress in 2007 legislated a return so low that no private lenders could make money holding these assets. To keep the money flowing to student borrowers, the government began buying the loans from private originators last year. But this larger federal role was intended to be temporary, with an expiration date next summer. The news from Washington now is that rather than scaling back federal involvement, the pols want the U.S. Department of Education to be the exclusive banker to America's college students.

4. *June 3, 2014, at Obama's Organizing for Action website, bullet points listed included "Rewarding responsible students— President Obama successfully fought to prevent federal student loan interest rates from doubling for more than 7 million students, and capped federal student loan repayments at 10% of income."*

5. *Obama aided the group that tried without success to revise U.S. history education in the 1990's to get a foothold with math and English. When offered a lump sum of money from the American Reinvestment and Recovery Act of 2009 (also known as [AKA] the Stimulus bill), 46 states, encouraged by their state governors, signed onto Obama's Race to the Top's Common Core State Standards Initiative authored by Achieve, Inc. Implemented in Fall, 2012, Common Core standards alter the math and English language arts standards of public schools' curriculums. English is for reading instruction manuals rather than great literature, and college preparation is for entering community college rather than university. Geometry is taught by a method that has not worked in the past. Teachers are not permitted to deviate and texts are constructed with the input of the U.S. Department of Education. Individual students' preferences or retention are not a consideration. Schools are instructed to compile and store data on students' test scores and ideally other data such as health history, family income and voter status. Sharing of data from state to state and federal government is done without parents' knowledge or consent because of the gutting of privacy laws. Achieve, Inc. "next generation science standards" were ready online July 10, 2012. Information on Common Core from presentation by Jane Robbins, Attorney, American Principles Project (americanprinciplesproject.org).*

6. *Obama's longtime associate Bill Ayers, a retired professor of elementary education in the College of Education at the University of Illinois at Chicago, known for co-founding "the*

Weather Underground, a self-described communist revolutionary group that conducted a campaign of bombing public buildings (including police stations, the U.S. Capitol Building, and the Pentagon) during the 1960s and 1970s in response to U.S. involvement in the Vietnam War" (quoted from http:// en.wikipedia.org/wiki/Bill_Ayers online), sits on the Board of Directors for two or three textbook publishers for Common core: "'The publishers of textbooks, schoolbooks really went from quite a few down to three or four basic publishers, and Bill Ayers sits on the board of directors for two or three of those,' Dendy said. 'Now what does that tell you? Of course the textbook publishers are promoting this Common Core because it would mean that they could produce the same textbook for the entire country.'" (Quoted from April 25, 2013 article by Jon Gillooly in The Marietta Daily Journal online).

Explanatory/supportive text
from Section 2 of the Communist Manifesto:

In bourgeois society, therefore, the past dominates the present; in Communist society, the present dominates the past . . . .

The Communists have not invented the intervention of society in education; they do but seek to alter the character of that intervention, and to rescue education from the influence of the ruling class . . . .

Nevertheless in the most advanced countries, the following will be pretty generally applicable . . . .

5. Centralization of credit in the hands of the State, by means of a national bank with State capital and an exclusive monopoly.

10. Free education for all children in public schools. Abolition of children's factory labor in its present form. Combination of education with industrial production, &c., &c.

2. Communist agenda: Destroy financial capital

Run the debt up to undermine the soundness of the money/ capital supply (the fastest way to destroy an advanced capitalist country).

Obama's actions

1. *Democrats assumed total control of the budget process on January 3, 2007, when they took the House of Representatives as well as the Senate of Congress for the first time since 1995. (January 3, 2007 the deficit spending was declining for the fourth year in a row, the unemployment rate was 4.6%, and there had been 52 straight months of job growth). Continuing to ignore President George W. Bush's requests, which totaled 17 since 2001, they failed to stop Fannie Mae and Freddie Mac's financial banking practices, and an economic meltdown occurred 15 months later. The U.S. government's budget is defined by the Federal Fiscal Year (FFY) which runs from October 1 of the prior year to September 30 of the numbered year, so the budget for 2008 was from October 1, 2007 through September 30, 2008. The budget process is that the President submits the next year's budget for consideration by the first Monday in February and Congress has until September 30 to approve it. FFY 2008 Congressional Democrats compromised with Bush on spending. FFY 2009 Democrats bypassed Bush with continuing resolutions until Obama became president January 20, 2009 and signed off on their massive omnibus spending bill to complete the 2009 budget.*

2. *The House of Representatives (AKA Congress) was won back by the Republicans in 2010 but not the Senate. Obama presented a budget for FFY 2012 with increased spending based on a projected increase in individual income taxes from 956 billion dollars in 2011 to 1,145 billion dollars in 2012 and corporation income taxes*

from 198 billion dollars in 2011 to 327 billion dollars in 2012, numbers so unrealistic that not even a Democrat in congress would vote for it in February 2011 (note page 174 of the 2012 Budget). To accommodate fed gov't's spending above intake of revenue and to prevent shutting down of the government's nonessential agencies, Congress raised the debt ceiling. That resulted in the first downgrade of U.S. government debt in history. Standard & Poor's cut its rating of long-term U.S. Treasury securities by a notch from 'AAA' to 'AA+' August 7, 2011.

3. *July 12, 2012, reported by Fox News online, "The U.S. budget deficit grew by nearly $60 billion in June, remaining on track to exceed $1 trillion for the fourth straight year. Through the first nine months of the budget year, the federal deficit totaled $904.2 billion, the Treasury Department reported Thursday. President Barack Obama is almost certain to face re-election having run trillion-dollar-plus deficits in each his first four years in office. . . . The International Monetary Fund warned that the U.S. economy could suffer another recession if Congress doesn't do something to avert the so-called 'fiscal cliff.'"*

4. *national debt increased from $15,000,000,000,000 plus in December 2011 to $17,000,000,000,000 plus in June 2014 per U.S. Debt Clock.org in real time online at http://www.usdebtclock.org/. Federal reserve is borrowing more than 40 cents of every dollar spent by the federal government from China, and other foreign countries, resulting in more and more tax dollars or percentage of gross domestic product leaving the USA to pay for the growing interest on the loans. The federal government continues to operate without a budget.*

5. *June 2014, the U.S. Bureau of Economic Analysis reported that the U.S. Gross Domestic Product (GDP) in the first quarter of 2014 went down 2.9% from the previous quarter. GDP averaged a 3.22% growth from 1947-2014.*

6. *Democrats block all efforts to become energy independent and*

stop the one way movement of U.S. money to other countries with oil. For example, April 2011, Obama, while ordering U.S. federal agencies to effectively stop offshore drilling with red tape, visited Brazil and encouraged them to drill offshore, assuring them that the U.S. "will be their best customer." November 2011, Obama delayed decision on construction of the Keystone XL Canada-to-Texas oil pipeline project until after the November 2012 election, in spite of the warning that Canada would turn to Asia to sell oil rather than wait on the pipeline. June 2014, Senate Majority Leader Harry Reid continues to block vote in U.S. Senate on House bill approving Keystone XL pipeline (see "Simulated Reserve and Corridor System to Protect Diversity" map for U.N. Agenda 21 at FreedomAdvocates.org).

7. *Summer 2011, Obama enacted "cap and trade" through federal orders for the Environmental Protection Agency (EPA) in support of U.N. Agenda 21 and against the will of congress (that is, the Republican majority in the U.S. House of Representatives). Congress opposed them because they will increase consumer utility rates and threaten continued U.S. coal mining.*

8. *gave through the Department of Energy over a billion dollars of taxpayer money from the 2009 $787 billion American Reinvestment and Recovery Act (AKA 2009 Stimulus Bill) to alternative green energy companies considered poor risk that eventually went bankrupt, including Solyndra, Solar One, Triad Ethanol Plant, Future Gen, and Clinch River Reactor. Also gave the taxpayer money to companies that outsourced it to countries outside the U.S.A. including England, Finland, China, and others (U.N. Agenda 21).*

9. *June 25, 2014, Republicans in the U.S. House of Representatives are trying to stop the continuation of the Export Import (Ex-Im) Bank. A bank that subverts the free market system by subsidizing a few government-picked companies such as Boeing and General Electric with tax payer dollars, it is the symbol for*

> *Crony Capitalism in America. Although Obama called it "little more than a fund for corporate welfare" September 22, 2008, he and other Democrats are fighting to renew it.*

Explanatory/supportive text

> *from Section 1 of the Communist Manifesto:*

The essential condition for the existence, and for the sway of the bourgeois class, is the formation and augmentation of capital.

3. Communist agenda: Encourage unhappiness worldwide

Encourage unhappiness with and disapproval of the existing world order.

Obama's actions

1. *did not condemn the president of Honduras for agitating for an unconstitutional 2nd term in 2009.*

2. *supported the plan for guns to Mexican drug lords with the allocation of $10 million from the 2009 Stimulus Bill to the Bureau of Alcohol, Tobacco, Firearms, and Explosives for the ATF Project Gunrunner (AKA "Operation Fast and Furious").*

3. *ordered the expenditure of $20.3 million in "migration assistance" for Palestinian refugees and "conflict victims" in Gaza with ties to Hamas to resettle in the United States.*

4. *hesitated to take sides on the revolution in Egypt (February 2011) or condemn the murder of antigovernment civilians in Iran (2009) and Libya (2011).*

5. *entered the conflict in Libya (March 2011) without consulting congress or seeking congressional approval.*

6. *signaled in his "Arab Speech" of May 19, 2011 that America is no longer Israel's guardian by stating that Israel's borders with a new*

Palestinian State would be the artificial and indefensible borders drawn by the United Nations in 1947 rather than the current ones in existence since Israel's defensive 1967 Six Day War.

7. *decided to formally resume contact (June 2011) with Egypt's Muslim Brotherhood, which does not recognize Israel, supports terror, and spreads hatred of the U.S. and Israel.*

8. *sent a letter to Congress Fri. Oct. 14, 2011 informing them that he had sent U.S. troops to Uganda (who arrived Oct. 12) and will send others to South Sudan, the Central African Republic and the Democratic Republic of the Congo to put down years-long insurgencies, going against the traditional reluctance of the U.S. to intervene.*

9. *failed to condemn the mass persecution of Christians in the Mideast after saying in April 2012 "where we once were we are no longer a Christian nation, at least not ' just,' we are also a Jewish nation, a Muslim nation, and a Buddhist nation, and a Hindu nation and a nation of nonbelievers."*

10. *Obama's visit to the leader of Turkey in June, 2013 was followed two weeks later by that leader violently suppressed peaceful protestors who were against his movement of the government from secular to Sharia law.*

11. *threatened but failed to act against Syrian government led by President Bashar al-Assad when they used chemical weapons against their own people in civil war (2013).*

12. *threatened but failed to stop Ukrainian officials from cracking down on mass protests (February 2014).*

13. *threatened to try to stop Russian government led by President Vladimir Putin from moving into the Ukraine and taking over the Crimean Peninsula (February 2014).*

14. *failed to negotiate an extension of U.S.-Iraq Status of Forces Agreement signed by President George W. Bush in 2008, beyond previously agreed upon deadline of December 31, 2011, so Iraq-stabilizing American military forces were completely withdrawn*

between June 2009 and December 2011.

15. *exchanged May 31, 2014 Army Sergeant Bowe Bergdahl for five extremely dangerous prisoners from Guantanamo Bay, Cuba. The "Dream Team Taliban Five" were reportedly handpicked by the Taliban for the trade. The exchange was made without the 30 day prior notice to the U.S. Congress required by law.*

16. *declined to prevent invasion in June 2014 of Iraq by the Islamic State in Iraq and Syria (ISIS), by declining to use drones to attack the ISIS army as it began to form up and cross the border per intelligence. ISIS is fighting to establish a Caliphate—an Islamic state inhabited only by the Muslim faithful, living under the Constitution of Medina and strict Sharia law, led by a supreme leader who is the caliph or successor to Muhammad. ISIS, with similar to Al-Qaeda global aspirations, intends to consolidate Iraq and Syria, threaten bordering countries Jordan and Lebanon, and breed terrorists to target such as the United States.*

Explanatory/supportive text

from Section 1 of the Communist Manifesto:

All previous historical movements were movements of minorities, or in the interests of minorities. The proletarian movement is the self-conscious, independent movement of the immense majority, in the interests of the immense majority. The proletariat, the lowest stratum of our present society, cannot stir, cannot raise itself up, without the whole superincumbent strata of official society being sprung into the air.

Though not in substance, yet in form, the struggle of the proletariat with the bourgeoisie is at first a national struggle. The proletariat of each country must, of course, first of all settle matters with its own bourgeoisie.

In depicting the most general phases of the development of the proletariat, we traced the more or less veiled civil war, raging within existing society, up to the point where that war breaks out into open revolution, and where the violent overthrow of the bourgeoisie lays the foundation for the sway of the proletariat.

from Section 4 of the Communist Manifesto:

In short, the Communists everywhere support every revolutionary movement against the existing social and political order of things.

4. Communist agenda: Destroy credibility of capitalists

Destroy the credibility of capitalists within the USA and around the world to decrease resistance to the new world order.

Obama's actions

1. *apologized for the United States on worldwide tour in 2009— see bow to the King of Saudi Arabia (*http://www.youtube. com/watch?v=9WlqW6UCeaY*).*

2. *does not act or follow through usually on the capitalist-like words he reads from his TelePrompTers.*

3. *demonizes Tea Party members (once known as the "Silent Majority" or taxpaying middle class) who unified to protest the government's failure to follow the Constitution and stop the freefall in our economy with free market solutions.*

4. *scraped a missile-defense agreement September 17, 2009 negotiated by the George W. Bush administration with Poland and the Czech Republic for mutual defense against a possible Iranian missile attack.*

5. *ended the three decade old National Aeronautics and Space Administration (NASA) shuttle program July 2011, making the USA dependent on other countries to take an American astronaut into space (e.g., millions of dollars to Russia per astronaut with no guarantee they will bring them home) and increasing the risk of threat and intimidation from other countries, for example,*

from satellite weapons.

6. *decided not to retrieve or destroy an intact, unmanned U.S. military drone with top secret technology that fell into Iran December 2011.*

7. *changed sides on same-sex marriage. His explanation, quoted on May 10, 2012 White House Blog "President Obama Supports Same-Sex Marriage," did not include any reference to God, Bible, Judeo-Christian teachings, or any faith.*

8. *failed to pressure Pakistan to free Dr. Afridi, imprisoned since spring 2012, for working with the CIA to find and kill Osama Bin Laden.*

9. *NextNewsNetwork published online on You Tube January 23, 2013 (http://www.youtube.com/watch?v=kzT6X3_Bg9o) an interview with Dr. Jim Garrow by Gary Franchi of WHDN Boston. Dr. Garrow, an expert on China, talks about our "debt that can never be repaid" to China in addition to Obama's new litmus test for keeping top military leaders–would they be able to follow their oath of office and fire on American citizens if they refuse to lay down their arms? Garrow describes how China has assessed our natural resources as payment for our debt and how they want America disarmed. He also discusses the Chinese perception of Obama as a traitor to his own country.*

10. *In a December 21, 2013 article for the World Socialist Web Site (wsws. org) published by The International Committee of the Fourth International (ICFI), entitled "Latest Snowden revelations expose Obama's lies on NSA spy programs," Bill Van Auken writes that "Just hours after receiving a report from his hand-picked advisory panel on National Security Agency surveillance operations, President Barack Obama used his end of the year press conference Friday to deliver an Orwellian defense of unrestrained US spying both at home and abroad. 'I have confidence that the NSA is not engaging in domestic surveillance and snooping around,' Obama said, despite the cascade of revelations proving just the opposite. These revelations, including* *the latest from former NSA contractor Edward Snowden, have established that the agency is collecting and storing billions of files recording the phone calls, text messages, emails, Internet searches and even the daily movements of virtually every US citizen, not to mention those of hundreds of millions of people abroad."*

11. *February 20, 2014 Matt Spetalnick published in Reuters online (reuters.com) in article entitled "Obama's Syria 'red line' has echoes in his warning to Ukraine" that "U.S. President Barack Obama's stern warning this week to Ukrainian officials was the closest thing to a 'red line' moment he has had since his threat in 2012 to act against the Syrian government if it used chemical weapons. But Obama's admonition on Wednesday to not 'step over the line' in cracking down on mass protests rocking the Ukraine raised questions on whether he would be any more effective at matching words with deeds than he has been in Syria's three-year-old civil war. His decision to lay down another rhetorical 'line' in a geopolitical crisis left many foreign policy experts puzzled, especially given the limited options he has at his disposal for dealing with the Ukraine's spiraling conflict. . . . Obama's choice of words evoked comparisons to the chemical weapons 'red line' he established for Syrian President Bashar al-Assad and then failed to enforce with military action last year, something critics say undermined U.S. credibility."*

12. *June 2, 2014 John Hayward posted in Human Events online (humanevents.com) an article entitled "Obama's illegal, and highly questionable, Afghanistan prisoner exchange." He wrote that "While it is almost universal for the media to describe this deal as a prisoner swap with the Taliban, the Washington Post article on the five released detainees very gingerly brushes past an important fact, about fifteen paragraphs in: Sgt. Bergdahl was not a prisoner of the Taliban. He was captured and held by the Haqqani terrorist network, a detail the Obama media seems oblivious to, since the White House hasn't programmed them to*

discuss it via talking-points memo." According to Wikipedia, the free encyclopedia online (Wikipedia.org), the Haqqani terrorist network is affiliated with Al- Qaeda, "The significant difference between the two organizations is that Al-Qaeda's goals are global and use global means; whereas Haqqani is solely interested in Afghanistan and the Pashtun Tribal regions. . . . more interested in the influence of Islamic Law over Afghanistan than the global Jihad . . . . Haqqani was not affiliated with the Taliban until they captured Kabul and assumed de facto control of Afghanistan in 1996. . . . their actions of providing safe-havens for Al- Qaeda and Osama Bin Laden shows the strength of bond and some role in or knowledge of Al-Qaeda and Bin Laden's escape."

13. June 3, 2014 Noah Rothman published online at Mediaite (mediaite. com) that "While in Poland on Tuesday, President Barack Obama was asked if the five Taliban prisoners released from Guantanamo Bay in exchange for U.S. Army Sgt. Bowe Bergdahl could eventually return to the battlefield in Afghanistan and pose a threat to American personnel or interests. Obama said that, while his administration does not believe these individuals pose an imminent threat, there is always the risk of recidivism from released Guantanamo prisoners. 'In terms of potential threats, the release of the Taliban who were being held in Guantanamo was conditioned on the Qataris keeping eyes on them and creating a structure in which we can monitor their activities,' Obama said. 'We will be keeping eyes on them.' 'Is there the possibility of some of them trying to return to activities that are detrimental to us? Absolutely,' Obama continued. 'That's been true of all the prisoners that were released from Guantanamo Bay. There is a certain recidivism rate that takes place.' 'I wouldn't be doing it if I thought that it was contrary to American national security,' the president concluded."

Explanatory/supportive text

from Section 1 of the Communist Manifesto: Modern industry has established the world-market, for which the discovery of America paved the way. . . .

has set up that single, unconscionable freedom -- Free Trade. In one word, for exploitation, veiled by religious and political illusions, naked, shameless, direct, brutal exploitation. . . .

The proletarian is without property; his relation to his wife and children has no longer anything in common with the bourgeois family-relations; modern industrial labor, modern subjection to capital, the same in England as in France, in America as in Germany, has stripped him of every trace of national character. Law, morality, religion, are to him so many bourgeois prejudices, behind which lurk in ambush just as many bourgeois interests.

from Section 2 of the Communist Manifesto:

There are, besides, eternal truths, such as Freedom, Justice, etc. that are common to all states of society. But Communism abolishes eternal truths, it abolishes all religion, and all morality, instead of constituting them on a new basis; it therefore acts in contradiction to all past historical experience.

5. Communist agenda: Promote dissatisfaction of working men and eliminate the middle class

Promote working man's dissatisfaction with the capitalist or "ruling class" (middle class) so they eliminate it.

Obama's actions

1. *not helping in job creation in the private sector but rather increasing the number of federal employees across the board, including requiring the hiring of 16,000 new Internal Revenue*

Service (IRS) agents for implementation of the health care reform bill of 2010, H.R.3590 The Patient Protection and Affordable Care Act (AKA PPACA and Obamacare).

2. *suppress the growth of small businesses by increasing regulations and operational costs ($1.7 trillion in 2010).*

3. *negatively impact the unemployment rate: reported as 8.2% for whites, 16.8% for blacks and 11.3% for Latinos in July 2011 (The New York Times September 2, 2011) and predicted by the Congressional Budget Office (September 2011) to be above 8% until 2014.*

4. *negatively impact unemployed Americans' job search and job change by extending weeks of unemployment benefits to years.*

5. *gave tacit (understood without being outwardly expressed) approval to the organizers of Occupy Wall Street (started September 17, 2011) to continue their protests and interference with businesses throughout America.*

6. *from 2007 (the year when Democrat Nancy Pelosi became Speaker of the House and pushed for spending over the federal budget) to 2010 virtually every American family's income and net worth declined according to the Federal Reserve Board's Survey of Consumer Finances. Families' mean income dropped 11.1% when adjusted for inflation and median income dropped 7.7%. Findings were reported June 16, 2012. The report is issued every 3 years.*

7. *used money from the 2009 Stimulus Bill in large part to shore up state governments and unions. He proposed an American Jobs Act for more stimulus money in 2011 which did not pass. "Many public sector employees already have seen their wage growth slow or grind to a halt — even fall after adjusting for inflation" reported the Christian Science Monitor online July 12, 2012. The states of Arizona, California, and Florida are no longer giving raises. Due to increasing debt, U.S. municipalities like Stockton, California; Vallejo, California; and Jefferson*

County, Alabama are bankrupt. San Bernardino, California and Mammoth Lakes, California are on the road to bankruptcy. The mayor of Scranton, Pennsylvania—prohibited from filing bankruptcy by the state—is being sued for paying city workers, including him, minimum wage ($7.25/hour).

8. *campaigned in 2012 for reelection by:*

   a. *promoting Marx's class warfare, that is, "you" are living poorly because "they" are living well, or in other words, "you" are losing your house because "they" are not paying their fair share in taxes.*

   b. *denigrating successful middle class entrepreneurs with statements like the one he made extemporaneously at a campaign stop in Roanoke, Virginia Friday, July 13, 2012 (begin quote) There are a lot of wealthy, successful Americans who agree with me because they want to give something back. If you've been successful, you didn't get there on your own. You didn't get there on your own. I'm always struck by people who think, well, it must be because I was just so smart. There are a lot of smart people out there. It must be because I worked harder than everybody else. Let me tell you something -- there are a whole bunch of hardworking people out there. If you were successful, somebody along the line gave you some help. There was a great teacher somewhere in your life. Somebody helped to create this unbelievable American system that we have that allowed you to thrive. Somebody invested in roads and bridges. If you've got a business, you didn't build that. Somebody else made that happen. The Internet didn't get invented on its own. Government research created the Internet so that all the companies could make money off the Internet. (End quote).*

   c. *dismissing criticizers through surrogates as "racists" or "protectors of the rich" and failing to address the merits of any criticism by making broad statements like the one he made on CBS news Thursday morning, July 12, 2012, "The mistake of my first couple of years was thinking that this job was just about getting the policy right, and, that's important, but the nature of this office is also to tell a story to the American people."*

d. *blaming the bad economy on former President George W. Bush ("it was worse than I thought") or capitalism ("it never worked") and pushing news media to pile blame on Wall Street for illegal insider trading and other misdoings. His media push cooled somewhat November 13, 2011, when the television program "60 Minutes" broke the story that elected officials had exempted themselves from the laws, and that House Majority now Minority Leader Nancy Pelosi used insider information that is illegal for the average citizen to trade with to purchase some very fruitful stock in Initial Public Offerings.*

e. *accusing Mitt Romney, the presumptive Republican presidential candidate for 2012, of sending jobs overseas or "outsourcing" because of his connection to Bain Capital. In the same years, 1999-2002, Obama accepted campaign contributions from Bain executives. And according to the July 16, 2012 report of his presidential campaign committee, the Obama Victory Fund, funds were raised for him in Geneva, Switzerland; Stockholm, Sweden; Paris, France; and (Communist) Shanghai, China.*

9. *promoting a welfare state by:*

a. *made it easier for jobless, childless adults to qualify for Supplemental Nutrition Assistance Program (SNAP) and used money from the 2009 Stimulus Bill to increase the SNAP monthly benefit by about 15% through 2013. The number of people receiving SNAP soared to an average 44.7 million in fiscal 2011 or 1 in 7 Americans, up 33% from fiscal 2009. (Some call Obama the Food Stamp or*

Entitlement President).

b. *promoted and then signed into law in 2010, H.R.3590 The Patient Protection and Affordable Care Act (also known as PPACA and Obamacare) which, as one of the largest tax increases in history, is blamed for the United States' worst economic downturn since the Great Depression, with flat to negative job growth in the private sector in the summer of 2012.*

c. *proposed July 12, 2012 welfare-to-work waivers for states— California, Connecticut, Minnesota, Nevada, and Utah expressed interest— which would in effect "gut" the 1996 law. Welfare to work was at the heart of the landmark 1996 federal welfare reform law signed by President Bill Clinton (Democrat), which replaced a federal entitlement with grants to the states. It put a time limit on how long families get aid and requires recipients to eventually go to work. The well liked program, called Temporary Assistance for Needy Families, cut welfare in half when it started.*

10. *WASHINGTON, Jan. 28, 2014 (UPI)—"U.S. President Obama used his State of the Union address Tuesday night to renew his call for a higher minimum wage. He said he wants to see the minimum wage raised to $10.10 an hour and 'Congress needs to get on board.' 'Today, the federal minimum wage is worth about 20 percent less than it was when Ronald Reagan first stood here,' he said, and raising the minimum will help families."*

Explanatory/supportive text

from Section 1 of the Communist Manifesto:

The modern laborer, on the contrary, instead of rising with the progress of industry, sinks deeper and deeper below the conditions of existence of his own class. He becomes a pauper and pauperism develops more rapidly than population and wealth. And here it becomes evident, that the bourgeoisie is unfit any longer to be the ruling class in society, and to impose its conditions of existence upon society as an over-riding law. It is unfit to rule because it is incompetent to assure an existence to its slave within his slavery, because it cannot help letting him sink into such a state, that it has to feed him, instead of being fed by him. Society can no longer live under this bourgeoisie, in other words, its existence is no longer compatible with society.

6. Communist agenda: Use trade unions

Promote trade unions because they upset/fight against the capitalist or "ruling class."

Obama's actions

1. *a proponent of "card check," so voting for or against unionization will no longer be done with a secret ballot.*

2. *bailed out and took ownership of automobile companies General Motors and Chrysler, "stiffing" or cheating the private investors but protecting and benefiting the unions (2009).*

3. *gave waivers to trade unions so they do not have to adhere to Obamacare.*

4. *actively supported Democratic party organized union demonstrations in Wisconsin and Ohio March 2011.*

5. *ordered the National Labor Relations Board to prevent Boeing from extending its company to the right to work state of South Carolina from the union state of Washington May, 2011.*

6. *announced that the Service Employees International Union (SEIU) agenda "is my agenda" (see video "SEIU's Agenda is My Agenda" posted YouTube August 23, 2009 at http://www. youtube.com/watch?v=aQ1NJaCtIkM). Obama acted at*

least once as an attorney for the Association of Community Organizations for Reform Now (ACORN) in Chicago, Illinois.

7. *According to factcheck.org, the Service Employees International Union's political action committee, SEIU COPE, spent more than $27 million supporting Obama's candidacy through ads and other election communications in 2008 and at least $30 million in 2012. In 2013, SEIU COPE spent $2.5 million on paid media "to pass commonsense immigration reform with a pathway to citizenship."*

8. *According to Wikipedia.org, "While Reid won the Democratic nomination with 75% of the vote in the June 8 primary, he faced a very competitive general election for the Senate in Nevada in 2010. Reid engaged in a $1 million media campaign to 'reintroduce himself' to state's voters. He defeated Republican challenger Sharron Angle in the election despite losing 14 of Nevada's 17 counties." After attending my uncle's funeral in Boulder City, Nevada, February 2011, I attended a large gathering of patriots meeting at a restaurant in Las Vegas. I asked them "Why did Senator Harry Reid just win here?" Their answer, "We don't know, all of the rest of the elections went Republican." Then I asked, "Why when people cast their ballot on the machine for Sharron Angle, did Harry Reid's name keep coming up?" Their answer, "SEIU maintains not only the gaming machines in Nevada but also the voting."*

Explanatory/supportive text

from Section 1 of the Communist Manifesto:

But with the development of industry the proletariat not only increases in number; it becomes concentrated in greater masses, its strength grows, and it feels that strength more. The various interests and conditions of life within the ranks of the proletariat are more and more equalized, in proportion as machinery obliterates all distinctions of labor, and nearly everywhere reduces wages to the same low level. The growing competition among the bourgeois, and the resulting commercial crises, make the wages of the workers ever more fluctuating. The unceasing improvement of machinery, ever more rapidly developing, makes their livelihood more and more precarious; the collisions between individual workmen and individual bourgeois take more and more the character of collisions between two classes. Thereupon the workers begin to form combinations (Trades Unions) against the bourgeois; they club together in order to keep up the rate of wages; they found permanent associations in order to make provision beforehand for these occasional revolts. Here and there the contest breaks out into riots.

Now and then the workers are victorious, but only for a time. The real fruit of their battles lies, not in the immediate result, but in the everexpanding union of the workers. This union is helped on by the improved means of communication that are created by modern industry and that place the workers of different localities in contact with one another. It was just this contact that was needed to centralize the numerous local struggles, all of the same character, into one national struggle between classes. But every class struggle is a political struggle. And that union, to attain which the burghers of the Middle Ages, with their miserable highways, required centuries, the modern proletarians, thanks to railways, achieve in a few years.

This organization of the proletarians into a class, and consequently into a political party, is continually being upset again by the competition between the workers themselves. But it ever rises up again, stronger, firmer, mightier. It compels legislative recognition of particular interests of the workers, by taking advantage of the divisions among the bourgeoisie itself. Thus the ten-hours' bill in England was carried.

Altogether collisions between the classes of the old society further, in many ways, the course of development of the proletariat. The bourgeoisie finds itself involved in a constant battle.

7. Communist agenda: Use socialists

Ally with socialists to achieve similar goals.

Obama's actions

1. *May 22, 2012, according to Brent Bozell's Media Research Center the story that 43 Catholic dioceses and organizations are suing the Obama administration in federal court over Obamacare's forcing religious institutions to cover contraceptives and drugs or devices to induce abortion under their health insurance plans was blacked out on the television evening news of ABC and NBC while CBS gave it 19 seconds.*

2. *May 16, 2014, Scott Whitlock reported from the Media Research Center that the Veterans Administration story (that up to 40 patients in Arizona died due to lack of care) got 32 minutes and 25 seconds from NBC, 28 minutes and 2 seconds from CBS, and 11 minutes and 28 seconds from ABC. "In addition to avoiding culpability for the White House, the networks got to the story late. The story broke on April 23, but NBC didn't get around to it until the May 6 Nightly News. CBS and ABC discovered the controversy for that day's morning programs" (http://www.mrc. org/media-reality-check/networksdevote-72-minutes-veterans-scandal-just-5-seconds-criticism-obama).*

3. *The Internal Revenue Service (IRS) began targeting conservative advocacy groups for Obama beginning in 2012. Media coverage per Brent Bozell's Media Research Center's I STAND FOR TRUTH! Petition (http://tellthetruth2014.com/irs-scandal-blackout/) site:*
   - *On August 2, FoxNews.com reported that House Oversight chairman Darrell Issa had accused acting IRS Commissioner Danny Werfel of blocking the committee's investigation. Network coverage: Zero.*
   - *On September 4, CNN's Drew Griffin reported that documents showed Lerner's original story blaming low-*

level employees was a lie. Network coverage: Zero.

- *On September 11, 2013 the Wall Street Journal exhibited how Lerner's own e-mails implied a liberal political agenda at work. Network coverage: Zero.*
- *On September 18, 2013, a front-page analysis published by USA Today confirmed the targeting of conservatives. ZERO seconds of coverage.*
- *At the end of March 2014, the New York Times noted that the House committee was still being frustrated by noncooperation from the IRS. Network coverage: Zero.*
- *And, an April 7, 2014 staff report by the House Oversight and Government Reform committee thoroughly demolished what remained of the notion that both sides had been targeted. Network coverage: Zero.*
- *Finally on May 7, 2014, The House of Representatives voted to hold disgraced IRS bureaucrat Lois Lerner in contempt of Congress. Total network coverage? 15 seconds on Good Morning America. Zero on CBS and NBC.*

Explanatory/supportive text

from Section 4 of the Communist Manifesto:

The Communists fight for the attainment of the immediate aims, for the enforcement of the momentary interests of the working class; but in the movement of the present, they also represent and take care of the future of that movement. In France the Communists ally themselves with the Social-Democrats, against the conservative and radical bourgeoisie, reserving, however, the right to take up a critical position in regard to phrases and illusions traditionally handed down from the great Revolution.

8. Communist agenda: Eliminate international borders

Eliminate international borders for one world government.

Obama's actions

1. *sued the state of Arizona to prevent enforcement of Senate Bill 1070 (passed in 2010), a bill to stop the uncontrolled drug and human smuggling from Mexico.*

2. *mandated the medical coverage of illegal immigrants in Obamacare, the only low income people in the United States truly not eligible for already available state Medicaid or federal Medicare.*

3. *promoted the Dream Act for legalization of illegal aliens, defeated by congress in 2010.*

4. *kept Immigration and Customs Enforcement (ICE) from deporting illegals for simply being in the U.S. illegally per ICE Director John Morton's memo June 17, 2011.*

5. *mandated a case-by-case review of over 300,000 illegals stuck in the federal court systems August 2011 (while waiting illegals can get work permits, jobs, free medical care and free food).*

6. *announced June 16, 2012 his Department of Homeland Security policy to allow young people who were brought to the USA as young children to be considered for relief from removal from the country or from entering into removal procedures (by selectively enforcing laws).*

7. *moved to shut down nine Border Patrol stations across four states. Fox News online reported July 11, 2012: "Critics of the move warn the closures will undercut efforts to intercept drug and human traffickers in well-traveled corridors north of the U.S.-Mexico border. Though the affected stations are scattered throughout northern and central Texas, and three other states, the coverage areas still see plenty of illegal immigrant activity — one soon-to-beshuttered station in Amarillo, Texas, is right*

in the middle of the I-40 corridor; another in Riverside, Calif., is outside Los Angeles. U.S. Customs and Border Protection says it's closing the stations in order to reassign agents to high-priority areas closer to the border."

8. *From article "Obama adds to list of illegal immigrants not to deport: Parents." published in the Washington Times online (washingtontimes.com) by Stephen Dinan on August 23, 2013 "The Obama administration issued a policy late last week telling immigration agents to try not to arrest and deport illegal immigrant parents of minor children—a move that adds to the categories of people the administration is trying not to deport. . . . A year ago. . . a policy granting tentative legal status to young illegal immigrants brought to the country as children, who call themselves Dreamers. That policy began accepting applications in August 2012 and as of the end of this July had approved legal status for more than 430,000 illegal immigrants."*

9. *From article "IRS pays illegal immigrants $4.2 billion while stalling Tea Parties" published on Fox News Politics online by Kenric Ward on October 22, 2013: "While harrying and stalling Tea Party groups seeking nonprofit status, the Internal Revenue Service mailed $4.2 billion in child-credit checks to undocumented immigrants. Critics say midlevel IRS bureaucrats continue to abuse the Additional Child Tax Credit program by dispensing $1,000 checks to families in this country illegally. 'The law needs clarification that undocumented immigrants are not eligible,' Sen. Charles Grassley, R-Iowa, told Watchdog. org in a statement. To make Congress' intent clear—that only legal U.S. residents are entitled to ACTC credits—Grassley cosponsored a clarifying amendment with Sen. Mike Enzi, R-Wyo. 'Unfortunately, the majority leader (Harry Reid, D-Nev.) cut off debate, so we weren't given the chance to offer our amendment,' said Grassley, the top Republican on the Senate Judiciary Committee."*

10. *From article "More children crossing U.S.-Mexico border alone" published on CNN online (cnn.com) by Nick Valencia on May 21, 2014: "Children make the arduous trek from Central America across Mexico by train or with the help of smugglers called 'coyotes,' officials said. Most often, the youths from Mexico and Central America try to cross the border in the Rio Grande Valley because it is the southernmost point of the United States for them to cross. 'People that live north have no idea what's going on down here, and if they did, they would be appalled by what the government is letting happen,' Cabrera said. 'It's resources. I understand we're in a fiscal crunch nationwide, but this is not a problem that we can fix for free. I know the official line is that we're at 70% apprehension, but it's really more like 30%. There's a strain on manpower,' he added."*

11. *From article "Obama Directs Officials To Lead Relief for Children Crossing Border: Coordinated Federal Response Will Attempt to House Children Apprehended Crossing Mexican Border" published in Wall Street Journal online (wsj.com) by Laura Meckler and Jeffrey Sparshott on June 2, 2014: "WASHINGTON—President Barack Obama, citing an 'urgent humanitarian situation,' on Monday directed federal officials to lead a relief effort in response to a surge in children trying to cross the U.S.-Mexico border by themselves . . . . While the White House painted the move in humanitarian terms, Rep. Bob Goodlatte (R., Va.), chairman of the House Judiciary Committee, blamed Mr. Obama's immigration policy for the rise, calling it an 'administration-made disaster.' 'Word has gotten out around the world about President Obama's lax immigration enforcement policies and it has encouraged more individuals to come to the United States illegally, many of whom are children from Central America,' he said."*

12. *From article "White House seeks extra $1.4B to address surge in children crossing southern border" published on Fox News Politics online by the Associated Press on June 3, 2014: "Last month, the federal government opened an emergency operations center at a border headquarters in South Texas to help coordinate the efforts and the Office of Refugee Resettlement, a division of the Health and Human Services Department, turned to the Defense Department for the second time since 2012 to help house children in barracks at Lackland Air Force Base near San Antonio . . . . about 1,000 children were being housed at the Texas base and as many as 600 others could soon be housed at a U.S. Navy base in Southern California."*

Explanatory/supportive text

from Section 2 of the Communist Manifesto:

The Communists are further reproached with desiring to abolish countries and nationality.

The working men have no country. We cannot take from them what they have not got. Since the proletariat must first of all acquire political supremacy, must rise to be the leading class of the nation, must constitute itself the nation, it is, so far, itself national, though not in the bourgeois sense of the word.

National differences and antagonisms between peoples are daily more and more vanishing, owing to the development of the bourgeoisie, to freedom of commerce, to the world-market, to uniformity in the mode of production and in the conditions of life corresponding thereto.

The supremacy of the proletariat will cause them to vanish still faster. United action, of the leading civilized countries at least, is one of the first conditions for the emancipation of the proletariat.

9. Communist agenda: Abolish private property

Abolish private property because it cannot be possessed by all, and those who get to have property obtain it by oppressing those who do not.

Obama's actions

1. *no support for tort reform to curb frivolous lawsuits with high legal fees that result in unnecessary and expensive defensive medicine by physicians.*

2. *no support for decreasing income/property/estate/inheritance/ death taxes that result in confiscation of property by the government/Internal Revenue Service (IRS).*

3. *bailed out and maintained two of the biggest players in the 2008 economic and financial debacle: Fannie Mae (FNMA - Federal National Mortgage Association) and Freddie Mac (a branch of the Federal Housing Administration [FHA] and US Department of Housing and Urban Development [HUD]). These two Democratic party sponsored enterprises intimidated mortgage lenders into giving people without collateral easy home financing, resulting in unpaid mortgages/property taxes and repossession of their homes/property by banks.*

4. *signed into law in 2010, H.R.3590 The Patient Protection and Affordable Care Act (AKA PPACA and Obamacare), insuring: a fictional "all" (several million people are left out); future cost control; future access control; and destruction of free market health care with its accompanying research, innovation, price competition, and excellence (read Turner and others' 2011 book <u>Why Obamacare Is Wrong For America: How the New Health Care Law Drives Up Costs, Puts Government in Charge of Your Decisions, and Threatens Your Constitutional Rights</u>). The law was made_constitutional by the Supreme Court when Chief Justice John G. Roberts Jr. deemed it a tax. Obamacare gives*

government control over 20% of the US economy with real time access of the IRS to individuals' checking accounts for collection of payments and penalties.

5. *authorized the Environmental Protection Agency's use of compliance order procedures with restrictive and expensive rules and regulations for individual property owners that require virtually any landowner to pay hundreds of thousands of dollars in permit fees for ordinary home construction work or face hundreds of thousands of dollars in fines and penalties. (See UN's Agenda 21 map of the United States).*

6. *According to the Federal Reserve Board's Survey of Consumer Finances report June 16, 2012 (done every 3 years) virtually every American family's income and net worth declined from 2007 to 2010 – years that coincided with Democrat Nancy Pelosi's leadership of the House of Representatives.*

Explanatory/supportive text

from Section 1 of the Communist Manifesto:

The proletarian is without property;

from Section 2 of the Communist Manifesto:

In this sense, the theory of the Communists may be summed up in the single sentence: Abolition of private property. . . .Of course, in the beginning, this cannot be effected except by means of despotic inroads on the rights of property, and on the conditions of bourgeois production; by means of measures, therefore, which appear economically insufficient and untenable, but which, in the course of the movement, outstrip themselves, necessitate further inroads upon the old social order, and are unavoidable as a means of entirely revolutionizing the mode of production. . . . capital is converted into common property, into the property of all members of society, personal property is not . . . .

These measures will of course be different in different countries.

Nevertheless in the most advanced countries, the following will be pretty generally applicable.

1. Abolition of property in land and application of all rents of land to public purposes.
2. A heavy progressive or graduated income tax.
3. Abolition of all right of inheritance.
4. Confiscation of the property of all emigrants and rebels.
5. Centralization of credit in the hands of the State, by means of a national bank with State capital and an exclusive monopoly.

10. Communist agenda: Take control of communication and transportation

Thwart the unfettered communication and urbanization needed by an advanced country/industrial nation and take control of communication, communicators, and transportation.

Obama's actions

1. *included a federal allocation of $8 billion in the 2009 Stimulus Bill for high-speed rail.*
2. *included a federal allocation of $7.2 billion in the 2009 Stimulus Bill to expand broadband for internet access to the rural areas of Montana, Minnesota, and Kansas at a cost of $7 million per existing household (Mike Huckabee on Huckabee Fox News television show 7/9/2011).*
3. *included a "bridge to nowhere" in California in his budget proposal of February 14, 2011.*
4. *obtained "kill-switch" authorization from the Federal Communication Commission (FCC) to pull the plug on the Internet (as Hosni Mubarak did during Egypt's February 2011 uprising) with the FCC voting 3-2 along party lines for the Net Neutrality Act 12/21/2010 effective 2/21/2011.*

5. *signed March 16, 2012 the Executive Order "National Defense Resources Preparedness" under the Defense Production Act of 1950 giving him power to take over civil energy/transportation and to draft for military and nonmilitary purposes during war or peace.*

6. *signed April 13, 2012 the Executive Order "Supporting Safe and Responsible Development of Unconventional Domestic Natural Gas Resources." This executive order gave him power over natural gas resources in the United States, that includes the government control of production or nonproduction of gas, and the control of the production and use of vehicles powered by the transportation fuel Compressed Natural Gas (CNG).*

7. *tightened control over the release of statistical data such as unemployment figures. Reported June 9, 2012 that journalists were ordered to remove their own telecommunications equipment as "Labor Department Forces Journalists to Use Government-Issued Computers."*

8. *signed July 6, 2012 the Executive Order "Assignment of National Security and Emergency Preparedness Communications Functions" giving him power to control all private communications in the country in the name of national security.*

9. *sent his deputies, House Minority Leader Nancy Pelosi and the White House Chief of Staff Jack Lew, following Supreme Court Chief Justice John G. Roberts Jr.'s decision to make H.R.3590 The Patient Protection and Affordable Care Act (AKA PPACA and Obamacare) constitutional by deeming it a tax, to be interviewed on Sunday July 1, 2012 television and deny that the individual mandate or "penalty on free riders" is a tax.*

10. *sent his deputy, United Nations Ambassador Susan Rice, following September 11, 2012 murder of U.S. ambassador Christopher Stevens, information officer Sean Smith, and Navy SEALs Glen Doherty and Tyrone Woods at Benghazi, Libya to be interviewed on Sunday news shows Sept. 16, 2012 and claim*

that murders resulted from a popular protest against a U.S.—made video rather than a pre-planned terrorist attack.

11. *From article "Records Show IRS and Elections Commission Colluded Against Conservative Groups" published in Newsmax online June 3, 2014 that the "House Ways and Means Committee . . . are calling on the IRS to release all communications between the agency and the FEC between 2008 and 2012. . . . tea party and other conservative groups were, on average, asked three times as many questions as progressive groups. And conservative groups were less likely to be approved for tax-exempt status and more likely to have their applications delayed."*

12. *sent elected and nonelected Democrats to Sunday news shows in 2013-4 to deny and/or blame Republicans for failures in the computerized launch of Obamacare.*

13. *sent elected and nonelected Democrats to Sunday news shows May 2014 to deny potential similarities between federally run Obamacare and federally run Veterans Administration (VA) healthcare—comparisons started when "News investigations have revealed at least 40 veterans died while waiting for treatment at the Phoenix VA Health Care System. According to whistleblowers, hospital leadership was aware of the secret lists, which were used to hide the long wait times from officials in Washington" (quoted from article "Whistleblower: Phoenix VA Hospital Destroying Evidence" published by C.J. Ciaramella May 2, 2014 2:45 in The Washington Free Beacon online).*

14. *sent his deputy, White House National Security Adviser (former United Nations Ambassador) Susan Rice, following May 31, 2014 exchange of five Taliban kingpins held at Guantanamo Bay for Army Sgt. Bowe Bergdahl, to be interviewed on Sunday news shows June 1, 2014 and incorrectly claim: that Bergdahl was a prisoner of war captured on the battle field; and Bergdahl's health required a swift deal, so Congress did not get the required 30 day notice from Obama. (On Fox News 6/4/2014, former*

Bergdahl platoon members explained how then Private First Class Bergdahl left his post, walking away "under his own will and conscience").

Explanatory/supportive text

from Section 1 of the Communist Manifesto:

The bourgeoisie keeps more and more doing away with the scattered state of the population, of the means of production, and of property. It has agglomerated production, and has concentrated property in a few hands.

from Section 2 of the Communist Manifesto:

Nevertheless in the most advanced countries, the following will be pretty generally applicable. . . .

6. Centralization of the means of communication and transport in the hands of the State. .

9. Combination of agriculture with manufacturing industries; gradual abolition of the distinction between town and country, by a more equable distribution of the population over the country.

11. Communist agenda: Overthrow capitalists

Overthrow the capitalists in power and install the proletarians "in the know" (AKA communists).

Obama's actions

1. *staffed his new White House administration in 2009 with more than 30 czars with far left and openly Communist backgrounds, using them rather than his congressionally vetted cabinet to plan and implement his agenda. Their number reportedly grew to well over 100 by May 20, 2012.*

2. *as a candidate Obama said in July 2008 that he wanted a "civilian national security force" that "would be just as powerful and well-funded as the U.S. military," funding for a sort of civilian army was in the middle of the health care reform bill in 2010, H.R.3590 The Patient Protection and Affordable Care Act (see Act Sec. 5210. ESTABLISHING A READY RESERVE CORPS).*

3. *signed New Year's Eve, 2011 the new National Defense Authorization Act (NDAA) allowing the U.S. military or a U.S. president to detain anybody anywhere indefinitely without trial for no reason so long as they say (not prove) you are suspected of terrorism; language excluding U.S. citizens was removed at Obama's request, so the privilege of the Writ of Habeas Corpus (Article I, Section 9, Clause 2 of the Constitution) to appear in public court to challenge the legitimacy of arrest and imprisonment is not allowed; and NDAA gives the U.S. military the power to conduct domestic anti-terrorism operations on U.S. soil, impacting the restraints on the military imposed by the Posse Comitatus Act (U.S. federal law passed June 18, 1878).*

4. *signed March 16, 2012 the Executive Order "National Defense Resources Preparedness," under the Defense Production Act of 1950, giving him power to take over civil energy/transportation and to draft for military and nonmilitary purposes during war or peace.*

5. *signed April 13, 2012 the Executive Order "Supporting Safe and Responsible Development of Unconventional Domestic Natural Gas Resources" giving him power over natural gas resources in the United States, including the control of the production and use of vehicles powered by the transportation fuel Compressed Natural Gas (CNG) and government control of production of gas (or nonproduction per Agenda 21).*

6. *reauthorized funding and requested new regulations permitting and overseeing the development of domestic drone technologies.*

May 10, 2012 Public Radio International (PRI) online reported: "Domestic drones could enhance surveillance but infringe on privacy. Unmanned aerial vehicles commonly known as 'drones' may become a regular part of everyday life in the United States. President Barack Obama has reauthorized funding and requested new regulations permitting and overseeing the development of domestic drone technologies. As part of the FAA Modernization and Reform Act of 2012, signed into law by President Barack Obama in February, the Federal Aviation Administration is required to write new rules for expanding the use of U.S. airspace by domestic drones. Up until this point, drones were primarily operated by the military and homeland security forces. Hobbyists who were interested in building unmanned planes were carefully regulated. By next week, the administration will have to propose new practices to stimulate licensing for some government drones."

7. *allowed Russians to participate in war exercises in the U.S.A. May 17, 2012 KRDO.com online reported: "FORT CARSON, Colo. - The Russians are coming - in fact, they're already here - but it may not be what you think. Twenty-two Russian army paratroopers are at Fort Carson for two weeks of training with the 10th Special Forces Group. The two nations' militaries have been conducting joint exercises for years, but U.S. officials say this is believed to be the first time Russian soldiers have trained on U.S. soil. The soldiers are training together on basic combat skills ranging from firing weapons to making parachute drops. It's the first step toward joint exercises in more complicated anti-terrorism operations. The training involves only unclassified weapons, and the Russians have U.S. escorts around the clock. U.S. soldiers are expected to go to Russia for similar exercises next year." Reports from other online sources included that the Russians took and held the Denver Airport, had Nebraskan accented English, and were arriving in greater numbers and staying longer.*

8. *stopping different states' efforts to prevent voter fraud. Reported May 31, 2012 by the Miami Herald online: "Justice Department ordered Florida's elections division to halt a systematic effort to find and purge the state's voter rolls of noncitizen voters" claiming that "Florida's effort appears to violate both the 1965 Voting Rights Act, which protects minorities, and the 1993 National Voter Registration Act -- which governs voter purges." July 10, 2012 Attorney General Eric Holder blocks South Carolina and Texas Voter Identification (ID) Laws on grounds of racial discrimination.*

9. *Obama's friendly exchange at the tail end of his 90 minute meeting with outgoing Russian President Dmitri Medvedev in Seoul, South Korea March 26, 2012 was picked up by hot microphones as reporters were let into the room for remarks by the two leaders. The actual exchange: President Obama: "On all these issues, but particularly missile defense, this, this can be solved but it's important for him to give me space." President Medvedev: "Yeah, I understand. I understand your message about space. Space for you..." President Obama: "This is my last election. After my election I have more flexibility." President Medvedev: "I understand. I will transmit this information to Vladimir." The incoming Russian President Vladimir Putin opposed the plan for deployment of U.S. missile defense interceptors and sensors in Europe. Seen together since, Presidents Vladimir and Obama "acted" unfriendly to each other.*

10. *failed to respond publicly to the encroachment of nuclear capable Russian bombers upon American airspace. Two incidents occurred in one month, the second on July 4, 2012. The following quotes are from the Washington Free Beacon online, and all were from the first half of 2012. February 14 "President Obama has ordered the Pentagon to consider cutting U.S. strategic nuclear forces to as low as 300 deployed warheads—below the number believed to be in China's arsenal and far fewer than current Russian strate-*

gic warhead stocks." June 26 "Russian strategic nuclear bombers threatened U.S. airspace near Alaska earlier this month and F-15 jets responded by intercepting the aircraft taking part in large-scale arctic war games, according to defense officials." June 28 "The U.S. Northern Command and joint U.S.-Canadian North American Aerospace Defense (NORAD) Command said two Russian bombers violated U.S. airspace near Alaska during recent arctic war games." June 29 "China's nuclear warhead stockpile is more than twice as large as U.S. intelligence estimates and could include as many as 3,000 warheads, according to a retired Russian general and former strategic forces commander." July 6 "Two Russian strategic nuclear bombers entered the U.S. air defense zone near the Pacific coast on Wednesday and were met by U.S. interceptor jets, defense officials told the Free Beacon." July 19 "Recent incursions into U.S. air defense zones by Russian nuclear bombers earlier this month were part of exercises that violated provisions of the 2010 New START treaty, according to U.S. officials."

11. had the Pentagon submit a heavily redacted report on China and its military capabilities to Congress. In an interview by Fox News July 13, 2012 over growing outrage on Capitol Hill over Pentagon cutting size of reports to Congress, Representative Buck McKeon, Chairman of the House Armed Services Committee, said "China just increased their spending budget over 12% while we are cutting a trillion dollars out of our defense budget." Report due March 1 per a law set in 2000 was received May 15. Last year's report was 79 pages, this year's 19 pages, and whole sections of last year's report were not in it this year. Explanation was that Pentagon briefers were told to limit reports to Congress to 15 pages to save money. Report cost $73,000 plus last year, $85,000 this year. Chairman McKeon sent a letter to Defense Secretary Leon Panetta asking him to change policy that "reeks of obstructionism, a lack of transparency, and is harmful to constitutionally mandated congressional oversight and national

security." Rep. McKeon said that no funds will be approved "except for urgent needs for war fighters until they contact us and change this policy." In an email to Fox News, "McKeon's office said three sections of the 2012 China report that are required by law were missing and that it failed to mention major developments over the past year, such as the test flight of China's stealth jet, the J-22, and the maiden voyage of its first major aircraft carrier."

12. *no known response by Obama to report by Bill Gertz online in The Washington Free Beacon, June 12, 2013 that "China has been quietly taking steps to encircle the United States by arming western hemisphere states, seeking closer military, economic, and diplomatic ties to U.S. neighbors, and sailing warships into U.S. maritime zones."*

Explanatory/supportive text

from Section 2 of the Communist Manifesto:

The Communists are distinguished from the other working-class parties by this only:

(1) In the national struggles of the proletarians of the different countries, they point out and bring to the front the common interests of the entire proletariat, independently of all nationality.

(2) In the various stages of development which the struggle of the working class against the bourgeoisie has to pass through, they always and everywhere represent the interests of the movement as a whole.

The Communists, therefore, are on the one hand, practically, the most advanced and resolute section of the working-class parties of every country, that section which pushes forward all others; on the other hand, theoretically, they have over the great mass of the proletariat the advantage of clearly understanding the line of march, the conditions, and the ultimate general results of the proletarian movement. The immediate aim of the Communist is the same as that of all the other proletarian parties: formation of the proletariat into a class, overthrow of the bourgeois supremacy, conquest of political power by the proletariat. . . . proletariat will use its political supremacy to wrest, by degrees, all capital from the bourgeoisie, to centralize all instruments of production in the hands of the State, i.e., of the proletariat organized as the ruling class; and to increase the total of productive forces as rapidly as possible. . . .

Nevertheless in the most advanced countries, the following will be pretty generally applicable. . . .

7. Extension of factories and instruments of production owned by the State; the bringing into cultivation of waste-lands, and the improvement of the soil generally in accordance with a common plan.

8. Equal liability of all to labor. Establishment of industrial armies, especially for agriculture.

12. Communist agenda: Dominate world

Acceptance of worldwide dominance by the communist party.

Obama's actions

1. *is silent or deferring to the United Nations on international affairs (2009).*
2. *reported Arizona to the United Nations Human Rights Council (August 2010) for immigration law S.B. 1070, implying Arizona is under United Nations jurisdiction.*
3. *sought approval of the United Nations and not congress before sending soldiers to Libya (March 2011).*
4. *took "a back seat" to the United Nations in USA's "kinetic military action" in Libya (2011).*
5. *stated in a May 19, 2011 speech that Israel's borders with a new Palestinian State would be the borders drawn by the United Nations in 1947 rather than the current ones.*

6. *working for small arms/gun control through the United Nations. October 14, 2009, Obama reversed United States policy on a treaty to regulate arms sales by backing launching talks. July 2-27, 2012, the United Nations' conference in New York City drafted a final version of the UN Arms Trade Treaty. If signed by the United States and ratified by the U.S. Senate, the treaty will have the force of a constitutional amendment and override the 2nd Amendment of the U.S. Constitution Bill of Rights, the Right to Bear Arms. September 25, 2013 Secretary of State (former Senator) John Kerry signed the United Nation's Arms Trade Treaty. The proposed Arms Trade Treaty would be a legally binding treaty tightening regulation of, and setting international standards for, the import, export and transfer of conventional weapons. According to Reuters, "the proposed treaty is opposed by conservative U.S. think tanks like the Heritage Foundation, which said last month that it would not restrict the access of 'dictators and terrorists' to arms but would be used to reduce the ability of democracies such as Israel to defend their people."*

7. *signed January 18, 2011 Executive Order 13563 "Improving Regulation and Regulatory Review" which states "that our regulatory system must protect public health, welfare, safety, and our environment while promoting economic growth, innovation, competitiveness, and job creation. In an increasingly global economy, international regulatory cooperation, consistent with domestic law and prerogatives and U.S. trade policy, can be an important means of promoting the goals of Executive Order 13563." This executive order gave international regulatory cooperation priority over domestic laws and regulations (U.N. Agenda 21).*

8. *sent delegation to Rio+20, United Nations Conference on Sustainable Development in Rio de Janeiro, Brazil, June 20-22, 2012 to discuss status of Agenda 21. In line with it, Obama*

signed Executive Order 13575 on June 9, 2011 establishing the White House Rural Council to " federally coordinate and implement environmental development locally in 'sustainable rural communities'" and Executive Order 13602 on March 15, 2012 establishing the White House Council on "Strong Cities, Strong Communities (SC2)."

9. planning (reported June 23, 2012) for the USA to sign the Land of the Sea Treaty (LOST), an "international agreement" ceding control of the high seas and ocean floor to an organization headquartered in Jamaica which calls itself the International Seabed Authority (ISA). A wholly owned subsidiary of the United Nations, the ISA will have the sole power and authority to issue "permits" for fishing and drilling and mining operations at sea. When globalists in the U.S. Senate introduced LOST 30 years ago, President Reagan said "No national interest of the United States can justify handing sovereign control of two-thirds of the Earth's surface over to the Third World."

10. realizing the Agenda 21 map of the United States for the United Nations, beginning in California where cities are on the verge of disappearing after going bankrupt in the summer of 2012 due to increasing debt, largely from union negotiated contracts for guaranteed job security, health care, and pensions.

11. June 3, 2014, quoting from climate page at Obama's Organizing for Action website (address http://ofa.barackobama.com/climate/?source=footernav) with the heading:

"President Obama said if Congress won't act on the issue, 'I will.' Say you will support President Obama's plan and take action in your own community now."

And the bullet points were:

The President's plan to combat climate change

- Create the first-ever EPA limits on how much carbon pollution U.S. power plants can create
- Double the production of clean energy in the U.S. by 2020

- Lead the international community to address global climate change
- Prepare the U.S. for the impacts of climate change

Compare and contrast Obama's 2014 plan to U.N.'s Agenda 21 plan for protection of the atmosphere in 1992 (following quote from <u>*Agenda 21: Earth Summit: The United Nations Programme of Action from Rio*</u>*, p. 74, Chapter 9):*

Agenda 21—Chapter 9
PROTECTION OF THE ATMOSPHERE
INTRODUCTION

9.1 Protection of the atmosphere is a broad and multidimensional endeavour involving various sectors of economic activity. The options and measures described in the present chapter are recommended for consideration and, as appropriate, implementation by Governments and other bodies in their efforts to protect the atmosphere.

9.2 It is recognized that many of the issues discussed in this chapter are also addressed in such international agreements as the 1985 Vienna Convention for the Protection of the Ozone Layer, the 1987 Montreal Protocol on Substances that Deplete the Ozone Layer as amended, the 1992 United Nations Framework Convention on Climate Change and other international, including regional, instruments. In the case of activities covered by such agreements, it is understood that the recommendations contained in this chapter do not oblige any Government to take measures which exceed the provisions of these legal instruments. However, within the framework of this chapter, Governments are free to carry out additional measures which are consistent with those legal instruments.

9.3 It is also recognized that activities that may be undertaken in pursuit of the objectives of this chapter should be coordinated with social and economic development in an integrated manner with a view to avoiding adverse impacts on the latter, taking into full account the legitimate priority needs of developing countries for the achievement of sustained economic growth and the eradication of poverty.

Explanatory/supportive text
from the end of Section 2 of the Communist Manifesto:
In place of the old bourgeois society, with its classes and class antagonisms, we shall have an association, in which the free development of each is the condition for the free development of all.
from the end of Section 4 of the Communist Manifesto:
Finally, they labor everywhere for the union and agreement of the democratic parties of all countries. . . .

WORKING MEN OF ALL COUNTRIES, UNITE!

Note: President Obama deviates from the Communist Manifesto in one way. Karl Marx wrote near the end of Section 4 that "The Communists disdain to conceal their views and aims. They openly declare that their ends can be attained only by the forcible overthrow of all existing social conditions." Obama's deviousness is explained by <u>Rules for Radicals: A Pragmatic Primer for Realistic Radicals</u>, copyrighted in 1971 by Saul D. Alinsky, a book Obama was photographed explaining on a black board in a classroom some years ago.

From the Holy Bible, King James Version, the New Testament, the 1st Epistle of Paul the Apostle to Timothy, Chapter 2, Verses 1 & 2:
"I exhort therefore, that, first of all, supplications, prayers, intercessions, and giving of thanks, be made for all men;
For kings, and for all that are in authority; that we may lead a quiet and peaceable life in all godliness and honesty."

So I earnestly prayed for President Barack Hussein Obama II to fulfill the oath he took before entering on the Execution of his Office, that oath being from the Constitution, Article 2, Section 1, [8]:

"I do solemnly swear (or affirm) that I will faithfully execute the Office of President of the United States, and will to the best of my Ability, preserve, protect and defend the Constitution of the United States." Amen.

The War Within America

With the Constitution as written, resolute Republican "Tea Party" perseverance in upcoming elections, and nonstop prayer, I believe that the United States of America can survive the current communist threat. The call has gone out for principled, united action by traditional and nontraditional Republicans who have not been permanently influenced by Democrats' past calls for "bipartisanship." But as in the past when there were grave challenges to the integrity of the United States, amendments to the Constitution are indicated.

1) A Balanced Budget Amendment

Congress is charged by the Constitution with the collection of taxes and payment of debts. As of December 2011, per the U.S. National Debt Clock: Real Time at www.usdebtclock.org, the USA was more than $48,000 per citizen and $130,000 per taxpayer in debt for a total of $15,000,000,000,000 and growing. June 2014, per the online clock the USA is more than $55,144 per citizen and $151,160 per taxpayer in debt for a total of $17,555,000,000,000, with the different debt components growing too fast to read. A Balanced Budget Amendment is needed to spur Congress to behave more responsibly, and the amendment should stipulate that representatives must balance the budget by cutting federal spending rather than increasing taxes.

2) Congressional Term Limits Amendment

Three (decreased from my first proposal for six when I was a candidate for the United States House of Representatives from the great state of Georgia in 2010) consecutive terms of two years for the House of Representatives and two consecutive terms of six years for the Senate.

Limiting terms will prevent career politicians from dominating Congress. Elections will be of more interest to constituents since they will not be able to rubberstamp their first choice indefinitely.

3) Official Language English Amendment

Living in Germany from 1975-7, I observed that persons in England, France, or Spain could not do business with each other or someone in Italy or Greece without an interpreter. Professional interpreters were usually proficient in 6 different languages. One of the greatest strengths of the United States is that someone in New York can phone someone in California, Hawaii, Alaska, or states in between and do business directly with them.

My best friend in high school in Niles, Ohio spoke just like me, but at home she spoke Italian (or "pig Latin" as she called it) with her parents who were immigrants from Naples. When I asked her how she did it she explained that she learned from her two older siblings (who were born in Italy) and in school. My friend went on to college and became a teacher of accounting.

We now have US citizens, born and educated in Atlanta, who cannot speak English. They will never achieve like my best friend did unless they learn English.

Stationed in Germany as an American soldier, I managed to work and live without speaking German. It was more time efficient to use the commissary for groceries and the base exchange for clothes at Ramstein Air Force Base. My friends and coworkers were American. Even though I lived "on the economy" away from the post, I, disappointingly, knew more German before I arrived in Germany than when I left.

Students' native languages should be used in our classrooms only to teach them English. Otherwise they will not have an equal opportunity to succeed.

4) Right to Privacy Amendment

Amendments 1, 3, and 4 of the 1st ten amendments (the Bill of Rights) protect privacy. Amendment 9 makes it clear that the Constitution does not specifically address every right retained by the people. Taken together Amendments 1, 3, 4, and 9 are known as the "penumbra," a shaded gray area of the Constitution that supports an unspecified but built-in or implicit right to privacy. "The concept of the privacy right 'penumbra' has informed many landmark Supreme Court decisions" (page 115, The United States Constitution: A Graphic Adaptation). With the advent of new technology_and threats, this right is in jeopardy and should be made explicit.

For example, Obama's Race to the Top's Common Core instructs schools to compile and store data on students' test scores and ideally other data such as health history, family income and voter status. Sharing of data from state to state and federal government is done without parents' knowledge or consent because of the gutting of constitutionally protected privacy laws since the federal government's USA Patriot Act (an acronym for Uniting and Strengthening America by Providing Appropriate Tools Required to Intercept and Obstruct Terrorism Act of 2001). President George W. Bush (Republican) signed the USA Patriot Act into law 10/26/2001 after 9/11/2001, when 19 suicide hijackers coordinated by the terrorist Islamic group Al-Qaeda led by Osama Bin Laden flew: American Airlines Flight 11 and United Airlines Flight 175 into the World Trade Center's North and South Towers in New York City; American Airlines Flight 77 into the Pentagon, the U.S. Department of Defense headquarters in Washington, D.C.; and United Airlines Flight 93 into a field near Shanksville, Pennsylvania, after its passengers fought back and deviated them from their path to Washington, D.C. Deaths totaled almost 3000 people from the attacks.

Another example is the domestic spying program, code named "Stellar Wind." Started post 9/11/2001 by the National Security Agency (N.S.A.) with warrantless wiretapping, it is the acquisition of "domain" activity on American citizens (banking, phoning, etc.) for query search later. The purpose of the profiles, built by graphing each domain and turning it into the 3rd dimension, is to monitor what people are doing. A large cooling facility in Bluffdale, Utah, just 20 miles south of Salt Lake City, can hold ten years of electronic intelligence gathered by the N.S.A. The law that oversees the N.S.A., the Foreign Intelligence Surveillance Act of 1978 Amendments Act of 2008 (also called the FISA Amendments Act of 2008), was extended December 28, 2012 until December 31, 2017 by a vote of 73 to 23 in the U.S. Senate. In the online video "NSA Whistle-Blower Tells All: The Program Op Docs The New York Times" (WRL 2) published August 29, 2012, Whistleblower William Binney warns that the United States is headed towards a totalitarian state like East Germany.

5) An amendment to clarify the 1st sentence in the 1st section of the 14th Amendment,

proposed on June 13, 1866 and ratified on July 9, 1868 to provide citizenship to former slaves and their children: "All persons born or naturalized in the United States, and subject to the jurisdiction thereof, are citizens of the United States and of the State wherein they reside." Clarification of this statement will discontinue the birthright citizenship of children born in the United States to illegal immigrants and visitors or nonresidents.

6) An amendment to repeal the 16th Amendment

proposed on July 12, 1909 and ratified on February 3, 1913 for income taxes: "The Congress shall have power to lay and collect taxes on incomes, from whatever source derived, without apportionment among the several States, and without regard to any census or enumeration."

The purpose of this confiscatory income tax, like all of the strategies listed by Karl Marx in section 2 of The Communist Manifesto of 1848 ("revolutionizing . . . . the most advanced countries . . . . 2. A heavy progressive or graduated income tax"), is the "Abolition of private property."

I prefer the consumption tax known as the FairTax to the flat tax, because the implementation of the flat tax would still require an Internal Revenue Service. However, either is far superior to what we have now.

7) An amendment to the 17th Amendment

(a progressive era amendment like the 16th) proposed on May 13, 1912 and ratified on April 8, 1913 for senators to be elected directly by the people rather than by their state legislatures. Federal interference/mandates to the states are wildly inappropriate, and they should be checked and balanced by state representation in the senate as intended by our founders. If senators were elected by state legislatures again, they would not be afraid to rein in entitlement programs that are bankrupting their states.

Proposed Convention of States

A case for a Convention of States has been made by attorneys Mark Meckler, co-founder of the Tea Party Patriots, and Michael Farris in the "USA Convention of States (ConventionOfStates.com): A Handbook for Legislators and Citizens." They state that "Rather than calling a convention for a particular amendment, Citizens for Self-Governance (CSG) has launched the Convention of the States Project to urge state legislators to properly use Article V to call a convention for a *particular subject*—reducing the power of Washington, D.C" (p. 4), and that the "most common objection to the Article V convention envisions a doomsday scenario in which delegates disregard the original issue, rewrite the Constitution, and change the entire American system of government" (p. 6). They argue that a Convention of the States is the safest alternative to preserve liberty.

My problem with their thesis is that most of today's citizens are ignorant of the U.S. Constitution and government. Our public educational system has, by design, been deficient for generations in that respect (witness the popular negative reaction to the Tea Party). For example, my formal education in communism consisted of practice drills in hiding under my desk when school administrators sounded the fire alarm to signal a nuclear bomb attack from the USSR/Russia. Today, American children are being similarly scared by movies about global warming and climate change. I was also shamefully ignorant about the Constitution, and many of our elected officials reveal their ignorance when they label the U.S.A. a "democracy" instead of a republic. At minimum they should say a "representative democracy" to distinguish it from a pure democracy.

I know that if I had not had personal contact with communism when stationed in Germany, I would not have been so alarmed by Obama's speeches. My memories worried me enough to pick up the Communist Manifesto for the first time in my life, educate myself, become active in politics, and even run for office. But because of the still deeply pervasive ignorance in America (witness the willingness of young teachers to indoctrinate our youngest children through the Common Core in socialism [see excellent article by Jennifer Burke, "Common Core Lesson Teaches that America is a Racist Nation," published by the Tea Party News Network tpnn.com, April 8, 2014]), I do not agree that a Convention of the States is the safest alternative today.

Obama's Iron Curtain / Blog
Posted March 29, 2012—ALL PATRIOTS MUST WAKE
UP NOW . . .

We American voters are responsible for our political leaders. Because we became complacent and went to sleep our government has slid away from the Constitution towards the Communist Manifesto. Preservation of our liberty by adherence to the Constitution is the responsibility of each and every freedom loving American. If we do not pass it on to our descendants it is our fault. The call is out now for the silent majority of taxpaying, hardworking Americans to become politically active without delay.

The Democratic Party embraced Socialists and Communists long ago. Because of "bipartisanship" many Republicans in the Grand Old Party (GOP) have been corrupted. But the Republican Party, started by people like Frederick Douglass and Abraham Lincoln to prevent the spread of slavery, is still our natural home.

Activism at the grassroots level is critical in the next election. ACORN Alinskyites now running Occupy Wall Street are counting on stealing votes in the next election. "Secret shoppers" are looking to start lawsuits against states that require voters to show identification, so they can have "provisional votes" which they intend to count immediately in spite of any legally specified delay. Check out the website www.truethevote.org online and do what you can to educate and motivate other legitimate voters. Know your neighborhoods so you can challenge votes attributed to unoccupied houses.

The "normalcy bias" kept Jews from escaping Nazi* Germany when they saw their fellow Jews disappearing. We need to break through our own "normalcy bias" before this coming election or it will be too late. Our republic will descend into a Communist dictatorship if our negligent complacency continues through the elections . . . The call has gone out for principled, united action by traditional and nontraditional Republicans. Please answer it by joining and becoming active in your local GOP organization today. Tomorrow is not just another day.

*Nazi: abbreviation representing pronunciation of first two syllables of Nationalsozialistische (Partei); a member of the former National Socialist German Workers' party, founded on fascist principles in 1919, headed by Hitler from 1921. (Definition from Webster's New Collegiate Dictionary, 1953, G. & C. Merriam Co., Springfield, Mass.).

Posted April 13, 2012—ABORTION IS TO COMMUNISM LIKE A HEADACHE IS TO A BRAIN TUMOR

In his manifesto Marx wrote "The bourgeois. . . hears that the instruments of production are to be exploited in common, and, naturally, can come to no other conclusion than that the lot of being common to all will likewise fall to the women. He has not even a suspicion that the real point is to do away with the status of women as mere instruments of production". . . In fact, the Communists did treat women like prostitutes when they came into power in Russia in 1919. All women became the property of the nation instead of private property by decree. A certificate issued to a working class man by his union entitled him to make use of a "nationalized" woman between 17 and 32 years old. Some Communist leaders advocated complete replacement of marriage and family by promiscuity (more about this on page 72, The Naked Communist by W. Cleon Skousen, 1958). With that mentality, support of all abortion as well as infanticide comes naturally to a communist (witness China and Obama when he was in the Illinois state legislature). That kind of mentality is also present in America at the Democrats' sponsored Planned Parenthood facilities. According to witnesses, Planned Parenthood personnel act like abortion is just another form of birth control, so their clients will return to them three or four more times.

Posted November 7, 2012—HOW DO YOU RECONCILE YOURSELF WITH A NATION THAT JUST SOLD ITS CHILDREN INTO SLAVERY?
The United States is $16 trillion in debt to nations and individuals worldwide. The president responsible for almost half of it with plans to spend more was just reelected. What collateral do you think he put up for that borrowing?

Posted October 17, 2013—THE SILENT MAJORITY IS NOW THE TEA PARTY
The Tea Party is the Silent Majority speaking. The Silent Majority, composed of hardworking, taxpaying American citizens who believe in the U.S. Constitution, is now shrinking due to Obama/Democrat strategies such as dumbing down education (see the Communist Manifesto), ruining the capital/ money supply (see the Communist Manifesto), and failing to secure borders (see the Communist Manifesto and the Koran). The Tea Party is the once Silent Majority.

Posted June 2, 2014—MY OLD ANSWER TO MY NEW QUESTION (Repeat post from April 27, 2012) Nancy Pelosi is the Democratic Party's Bellwether

"A leader of a thoughtless crowd" or "A wether, or male sheep, which leads the flock, with a bell on its neck" (definition from <u>Webster's New Collegiate Dictionary</u>, 2nd edition, copyright 1953). Nancy Pelosi, former Speaker of the_House of Representatives, is the Democrats' bellwether. She always addresses her followers like they are slow sheep and expects them to believe her without question. Tip: Whenever you hear her speak, substitute the word Democrats every time she says the word Republicans. For example, when she says that "Republicans are attacking the middle class," the truth is that "Democrats are attacking the middle class." In this way, you get the best insight into what the Democratic Party is actually planning or doing.

(Today's Question)
New Question: Why are Democrats and some political class Republicans destroying the middle class by following UN Agenda 21 (that is: exporting their jobs/companies to developing countries, increasing their cost of living expenses by withholding water and energy resources, and devaluing their dollars/savings through increasing federal government debt)?

Old Answer: Defense, ingenuity, and generosity of the U.S.A. are dependent on a large working middle class paying taxes on their earnings from labor and property. So, since the Democrat socialists/communists want to abolish the U.S. Constitution and have one world government, they go after/ attack the middle class. Eventually the system will collapse when the payers are gone, and all will be stuck with whatever the remaining dictatorial, socialist/ communist government class will allow them to have.

Posted June 2, 2014—INSIDE RUNNING FOR CONGRESS
I signed and mailed to the Federal Election Commission (FEC) the forms to restart my 2010 "Vann for Congress" committee December 7, 2013 (Pearl Harbor Day's 72nd anniversary). My address in District 8, Georgia qualified me to run for the U.S. House of Representatives from any district within the state, and I chose District 12. I ran as a candidate in the Republican Primary against the pseudo conservative, Southern "blue dog" Democrat, Representative John Barrow until another good Republican won the primary May 20, 2014.
To qualify for my committee's FEC number in 2010 (but not 2014), I had to spend (or be given) $5000 to prove that I was a serious candidate. To be on the primary's ballot, I had to pay 3% of the

representative's salary ($5220 in 2014) at the state capitol in Atlanta during the week of qualifying. My committee in 2010 and 2014 was a committee of one— myself—as chair, treasurer, and member (working together could not have been easier). I confess that if I had won either primary, I would have been seeking more help.

To run for congress (House and Senate) or president, showing one's birth certificate, picture identification, or social security number is not required. In contrast, to enlist in the U.S. Army Student Nurse Program at University of Nebraska Medical Center, Omaha in 1972, I had to have 3 references and the bureau of investigation for the military visited my home in Niles, Ohio and interviewed my neighbors.

Publication of political press releases is not required, but publication of paid political ads is. The following paid political ad appeared Wednesday, May 7, 2014 in the daily papers of District 12 and the Atlanta Journal-Constitution.

Georgia should hold an Advisory Referendum on whether the leadership of the U.S. Government should be impeached

Diane Vann, Candidate for Georgia District 12, U.S. House of Representatives, requests that Georgia include an Advisory Referendum on the ballot in the general election on November 4, 2014 asking voters if they support the impeachment of Senate Majority Leader Harry Reid, House of Representatives Minority Leader Nancy Pelosi, and President Barack Obama, since evidence exists that they are not upholding and defending the Constitution per their oath of office but are de-developing the United States by following the United Nations Agenda 21 of 1992 (documented by Dr. Ileana Johnson Paugh in "U.N. Agenda Environmental Piracy") and the Communist Manifesto of 1848 (documented by Diane S. Vann in "Undermining the U.S. Constitution").

Paid for by Vann for Congress
(Unfortunately, only the constituents of Harry Reid and Nancy Pelosi, in the states of Nevada and California respectively, can remove them altogether from congress). For a referendum to be included on the state of Georgia's ballot, the state's House of Representatives must request it.

From my campaign's push card ("Vann Like a Moving Van" bookmark) Like most of the Silent Majority I was drawn to the Tea Party after the leadership of the House of Representatives passed to Democrat Nancy Pelosi in 2007. As Speaker of the House she began the push for congress to ignore their fiscal watchdog responsibilities. Unable to approve any of Obama's submitted budgets because of their "funny numbers," Congress was **forced** to "approval" his unfettered spending by passing continuing resolutions and raising the debt ceiling. Collateral for the massive debt cannot help but be our children's economic freedom and probably our government-owned land's natural resources.

The U.S. Constitution, which provides for its own improvement through the amendment process, is an unparalleled foundation for any government in the world. It is based on Judeo-Christian beliefs: that family, laws, morals, and religion are important to all and should be upheld; and that one's ends do **not** justify means like lying, cheating and stealing.

The Communist Manifesto is the opposite of the Constitution. The Constitution is a prescription for building an advanced country, while the Communist Manifesto is one for bringing it down.

The leadership of the Democratic Party is now following the Communist Manifesto and not the Constitution. . . . If elected, I pledge to work to undo their intentional damage to the integrity of the United States of America.

Atlanta Press Club 12th Congressional District (Republican) debate Sunday, May 11, 2014 6:00pm
http://www.gpb.org/election-2014/atlanta-press-club/debate/republican/congressional-district-12

Debate 56:51 minutes, the following excerpt from 17:43-18:47 minutes

Nick Lulli: Sure, this question is for Miss Vann again, with your nursing background, I'm curious as to your take and opinion on the current health care situation in the United States.

Diane Vann: Well, I've been a nurse since 1974, registered nurse since 1974, and I believe that the problems really are within this medical system itself in that the prices were going up, up, up and because 3rd party payer was handling the payment of it, people were not really looking hard at their cost, and saying to that doctor "You don't have to order that X-ray just because you think I'm going to sue you. You don't have to do that defensive medicine with me," which now went up to about half the cost of our medical care. So in the event when you go after the people that are able to handle the payment, which is what Obamacare does, it doesn't handle the price, it just goes after the people able to pay it, you are going to collapse the system, eventually the system will be collapsed because those payers will be gone . . . so you'll be stuck with whatever (care) the government will allow you to have. . .

May 10, 2019
From the chapter "Constitution versus Communist Manifesto: The War Within America," the following was removed:

2) The Equal Rights Amendment (ERA)
Its entire text as written in 1972 is:

Section 1. Equality of rights under the law shall not be denied or abridged by the United States or by any state on account of sex.

Section 2. The Congress shall have the power to enforce, by appropriate legislation, the provisions of this article.

Section 3. This amendment shall take effect two years after the date of ratification.

Muslim settlements in the U.S. (more than thirty) have grown by leaps and bounds as family immigrated to live with family (e.g., Dearborn, Michigan and more recently Savannah, Georgia). Some American Muslims are pushing their communities to let Muslim Sharia law take precedence over local and state laws. The laws supporting equal rights that have passed and are currently proposed are not enough protection for women from this threat. The Equal Rights Amendment should be added to the Constitution as soon as possible.

I removed it because the laws for protection of women are now there, they just need to be enforced. And, thanks to Democrats, the current day interpretation of equal rights is to remove protection rather than preserve it. (For more explanation, read "A Pediatrician Explains How 'Dangerous' Equality Act Would Force Doctors to 'Do Harm'" social commentary by Katrina Trinko and Daniel Davis in The Daily Signal posted online May 10, 2019 at dailysignal.com).

Social Justice vs Social Injustice

Social Justice is a Myth
January 31, 2017

Social justice is a myth. For it to be possible, both mental and physical justice must exist, and they do not. Intelligence quotient (IQ) and physical prowess (for example, good throwing ability and coordination depends on having same sided eye and hand dominance) are God given and vary from child to child. The extremist socialist NAZIs* of World War II knew they both were essential, as evidenced by how they attempted to achieve mental and physical justice by exterminating people with lower IQs and physical infirmities in their gas chambers.

Social Injustice is Not a Myth
April 10, 2024

Social injustice is not a myth. It is humans discriminating unfairly against other humans. Examples of it include when the best qualified applicant for a job or promotion does not get it: because of their own race, sex, ethnicity, or physical status; or because a program such as Diversity, Equity, and Inclusion (DEI) mandates the selection of another applicant's race, sex, ethnicity, or physical status.

*NAZI "a member of the National Socialist party of Germany; a German Fascist." (Definition from Webster's Collegiate Dictionary 5th Ed., 1940, G. & C. Merriam Co., Springfield, Mass.).

SOCIALISM/COMMUNISM STATUS CODE RED

Layman's Definition of a Communist: "A Socialist with a Gun" (origin unknown) ATHEISTS' REACTION TO THE UNITED STATES (U.S.) CONSTITUTION — SOCIALISM/COMMUNISM

The U.S. Constitution is grounded on the Declaration of Independence, the document signed in <u>1776</u> which rejected England's control of America including taxation and <u>declared</u> all Men are created <u>equal</u> (with no limit on race, religion or culture specified) and "endowed" by their <u>Creator</u> with "unalienable" or non transferable <u>Rights</u>, that among these are #1 <u>Life</u> (with no limit on age or location), #2 <u>Liberty</u> (signers, who needed unity for revolt against England, unwilling to go ahead and dissolve slavery—see *U.S. Constitution Article IV* 1789 & *Amendment XIII* ending slavery following Civil War 1865), and #3 <u>Pursuit of Happiness</u> (selected happiness as #3 instead of private property); and that <u>Governments</u> are "instituted" or established to secure these Rights and derive their just <u>Powers from the Consent of the Governed</u>. Activation and implementation of the U.S. Constitution in <u>1789</u> produced an independent, self governing population and "capitalism."

The Merriam-Webster Dictionary online June 10, 2022 definition of CAPITALISM: "an economic system characterized by private or corporate ownership of capital goods, by investments that are determined by private decision, and by prices, production, and the distribution of goods that are determined mainly by competition in a free market."

Capitalism produces a middle class ranging from those living independently on weekly wages to those accumulating great wealth. Christian belief inspires those that can to assist those in the lower or below poverty class. Politicians are servants of the people and not a "ruling" upper class.

Writing "Undermining the U.S. Constitution," I realized that I could write a similar book during the term of office of any past or future president of the United States. Threats from people with evil agendas, within and from outside the United States, even within the White House, are continuous. Defending the U.S. Constitution, preferably without physical warfare, is ongoing.

EARLY SOCIALISTS/COMMUNISTS

1825 Robert Owens -- Born in Wales, an atheist, Owens purchased New Harmony, Indiana to create a utopian community. New Harmony changed American education, starting a new coed public school system. The socialist community failed in 2 years. Owens returned to London in 1828. Some of his family remained in the United States. 1848 Friedrich Engels and Karl Marx -- Both Germans from well to do families, both atheists, co-authored the Communist Manifesto in England.

SOCIALIST/COMMUNIST SUCCESSES in U.S.
Noted in My Lifetime

1960's Engaged in Vietnam War and subsequent wars as recommended in the Communist Manifesto of 1848. Educated the educators for grade schools to remove Civics courses (social science dealing with the rights and duties of citizens) and the Bible and prayer. Started passing legislation state by state for no fault divorce, beginning the replacement of fathers supporting their families with government-support to single mothers with children, thus destroying families and diminishing the man's role as breadwinner.

1973 Roe versus Wade legalized induced abortion via an

unconstitutional "Women's right to choose." Ramifications intended and realized included: denigrating/belittling female role of motherhood, male role of fatherhood, and parents' responsibility for nurturing, teaching, and protecting the innocence of their children. Necessitated starting the removal of the contradictory Hippocratic Oath to "do no harm" from medical schools' curriculum.

1986 H.R.5546 - National Childhood Vaccine Injury Act of 1986 (created the National Vaccine Injury Compensation Program [VICP], a no-fault alternative to the traditional tort system) and following court case resulted in pharmaceutical companies no longer being held liable for death/adverse effects from vaccines on the childhood vaccination schedule.

1992 At the U.N. Conference on Environment & Development in Rio de Janeiro, Brazil, the United Nations (U.N.) produced "Agenda 21" for "sustainable development." President George H. W. Bush (Republican), saying "It is the sacred principles enshrined in the UN Charter to which the American people will henceforth pledge their allegiance," signed it, along with 178 countries, as a legally non-binding statement of intent and not a treaty requiring ratification by the United States Senate. (U.N. Agenda 21: Environmental Piracy, Dr. Ileana Johnson Paugh). President Bill Clinton (Democrat) signed Executive Order No. 12852, "President's Council on Sustainable Development," June 29, 1993,(WRL 46), which enabled the executive branch to begin the process of implementing Agenda 21 as "soft law." Read more about this Communist Manifesto of 1992 on the Agenda 21 page of dianevann.com (WRL 47).

2000 Turned elections by "consent of the governed" into selection via precoded and hackable electronic voting machines.

Video "of computer programmer Clinton Eugene Curtis testifying under oath in front of the U.S. House Judiciary claiming that he was hired by authorities to help rig the outcome of U.S. elections. Curtis told the court in 2000 that he was hired by Congressman

Tom Freeny [sic] to build prototype software that would allow authorities to push the results to a 51/49 outcome if needed" (WRL 30) and (WRL31).

2010 Capped off the dumbing down of reading, writing, and arithmetic begun in the 1900's with the introduction and acceptance of "Common Core" into government funded public schools. Replaced printed textbooks with online computer learning, enabling the revision of history and definitions with no paper trail. Introduced a critical theory, Critical Race Theory (CRT), to blame social problems on social structures and cultural assumptions rather than individuals like President Woodrow Wilson and Planned Parenthood founder Margaret Sanger. CRT's focus on past racism within America teaches young Americans at best to disrespect the United States and at worst racism and to re-segregate, shutting people out on the basis of a superficial characteristic like skin color was and is un-Christian, un-American, and un-Constitutional. Destroyed or relocated statues of historic American figures whose private property included slaves, reminiscent of what the Chinese Communists did to destroy all reminders of history when they took over China in the 1900's.

2018 Fascism was Socialism 2.0, by Wallace Garneau, June 18, blog, The Daily Libertarian (WRL 4).

Quote:

When Benito Mussolini came to power in Italy, in 1922, he looked over at the Soviet Union and realized that communism had a fatal problem. Mussolini realized that any system based on a socialist structure had the same fatal flaw: socialism concerns itself with the distribution of goods only, with the flawed assumption that production will not change even when incentives do. . . .

Without profit as an incentive, the only incentives left were the whip and the chain. . . . Just societies elevate the importance of each individual. It is evil to treat people like farm animals, and as such, socialism is inherently evil. But Mussolini was not concerned with people as individuals, so the moral problem inherent to socialism was lost on him. . . . To the true socialist, all of the wealth created by production should go to the workers. Having private ownership profit from production is considered theft. D'Annunzio reasoned that under fascism, profit was not a problem, as anytime a private business person earned excessive profit, the fascist leader could simply seize it, and if necessary replace the owner with someone who was not as greedy. The quest for profit would, however, solve the problem of incentives. . . . Franklin Delano Roosevelt was so impressed with Mussolini's fascist state that he sent envoys to Italy to determine what America would have to do to bring fascism to the United States. Fascism would have been blatantly unconstitutional here, and Roosevelt knew it, but Roosevelt was very much a fascist, and he tried to increase the Supreme Court from nine justices to fifteen. Roosevelt would have appointed the additional six justices himself, and along with existing justices who were sympathetic to fascism, Roosevelt's court would have ruled fascist powers Constitutional. . . .

There were a lot of fascist leaders in the 1930's and early 1940s. Today we look at fascism as being racist, but the only openly racist fascist was Hitler. . . . for every Roosevelt there is a Hitler. Furthermore, power corrupts, making it very difficult for a benevolent leader to stay benevolent. Good dictators are the exception. Bad dictators are the norm. . . . What is clear is that our government already has far too much control over our economy, that our media is deeply biased in favor of state control (and there is currently no such thing as 'news'), and that a sizeable part of the public wants to head deeper into fascism. . . .

I don't believe our future is Socialism 2.0. I believe it is Socialism 3.0, which is nothing more than fascism without nationalism, and unless we want to be treated like farm animals, we need to fight that future together. End Quote
2019

Unethical pharmaceutical companies and doctors (medical/surgical/psych) manufactured pseudo sex changes (sex chromosomes in every cell are suppressed but not eliminated) that render transgenders sterile.

26 May 2019 Video "Behind the Push for Open Borders" Epoch Times communist expert Trevor Loudon: "This is an orchestrated, communist assault on America to destroy America's borders, to create confusion in America, to overwhelm the system politically. . . . You could have 3, 4, 5 million people trying to get in." (WRL 5)

29 May 2019 Article "Bilderberg Meeting 2019: Nothing to See Here; Move Along" Bob Adelmann Quote: gathering of some 130 wealthy and influential people in Montreux, Switzerland. . . . meetings operate under Chatham House rules, the first clue linking the group to the international deep state seeking to impose world government on unsuspecting citizenry. . . . Those rules allow a participant to attend the meetings, but he or she may not reveal the identity or the affiliation of the speaker or any other participant. . . . virtually every attendee . . . an enemy of national independence and a proponent of globalism and the ongoing global effort to undermine national sovereignty. . . agenda . . .

"A Stable Strategic Order" to be imposed upon unsuspecting citizens until it becomes futile to resist. There's "What's Next for Europe," a detailed discussion of how to integrate the EU into other regional affiliations on the way to world government. There's "Climate Change and Sustainability," the movement that justifies more and more government control over people as the faux solution to a faux problem. There's "The Future of Capitalism" segment, urging attendees to continue to work to move control of capital from private hands—probably not from their hands, though—to the tender mercies of the state. . . .efforts that began in 1954 . . . to build their brave new world. End Quote (WRL 6)

2020

26 April 2020 Article "'Dr. Fauci Gave $3.7 Million to Wuhan

Laboratory... Something Is Going On'—Rudy Giuliani Drops a Bomb on NIAID Director Dr. Tony Fauci" Quote: Back in 2015 the NIH under the direction of Dr. Tony Fauci gave a $3.7 million grant to the Wuhan Institute of Virology. . . . As early as 2018 US State Department officials warned about safety risks at the Wuhan Institute of Virology lab on scientists conducting risky tests with the bat coronavirus. US officials made several trips to the Wuhan laboratory. Despite the warnings the US National Institute of Health (NIH) awarded . . . grant. . . . growing confidence that the current coronavirus strain may have accidentally escaped from the Wuhan Institute of Virology rather than from a wildlife market, as the Chinese Communist Party first claimed. . . . "Back in 2014, the Obama administration prohibited the U.S. from giving money to any laboratory, including in the U.S., that was fooling around with these viruses. . . . Despite that . . . even after the State Department issued reports about how unsafe that laboratory was, and how suspicious they were in the way they were developing a virus that could be transmitted to humans," he claimed. End Quote (WRL 7)

U.S. federal agency under Dr. Anthony Fauci sent money to do gain of function research in Wuhan, China. Biological (bio) weapon COVID-19 (coronavirus [SARS-COV-2] 2019) created and leaked from Wuhan lab December 2019. Faux vaccines containing modified bioweapon with Wuhan spike protein (starts deadly clotting cascade in inflammatory response) made by pharmaceutical companies, sold and distributed worldwide (see 28 June 2022 and 24 November 2022). In the U.S both medical and military personnel mandated to take vaccines or lose their jobs.

"America's Frontline Doctors 1st Summit Washington, DC July 27, 2020" (WRL 48)

"Dr. Immanuel said it all, do not take the Vaccines" December 22, 2020 (WRL 49)

Links to additional videos at (WRL 26).

November 2020 U.S. President Donald Trump, a nationalist, lost bid for re-election to CCP pick Joe Biden. (WRL 27)

1 December 2020 Article "Firm That Owns Dominion Voting Systems Received $400 Million From Swiss Bank Account Funded by Communist Chinese Gov & Companies Before Election: Dominion Voting Systems has financial ties to the Chinese government, according to filings". (WRL 8)

Communist Manifesto of 1992, UN's Agenda 21, morphed into "The Great Reset" or Communist Manifesto of 2020

The Great Reset website Quote: WHY DO WE NEED TO RESET? The pause during lockdown created by the pandemic resulted in a 7% decrease in global emissions in 2020. The UN states that we need a decrease of 7.6% every year until 2030 to avoid climate and ecological disaster. . . . The Great Reset is a creative industry movement to embed the positive environmental shifts that have happened during lockdown as THE new normal. . . . The Great Reset is brought to you by Purpose Disruptors" End Quote (WRL 9)

The Great Reset World Economic Forum website "COVID-19: The 4 building blocks of the Great Reset" Quote: "The pandemic represents a rare but narrow window of opportunity to reflect, reimagine, and reset our world"- Professor Klaus Schwab, Founder and Executive Chairman, World Economic Forum. Follow insights on how we can recover from COVID-19 to build a healthier, more equitable, and more prosperous future. . . . ENTREPRENEURSHIP How digital entrepreneurs will help shape the world after the COVID-19 pandemic Brian A. Wong 04 Jun 2020 End Quote (WRL 39)

2021

12 Feb 2021 Video "The Web of Players Trying to Silence Truth" Dr. Joseph Mercola (WRL 10)

Quote: The Publicis Groupe, a leading PR firm, represents major companies within the technology, pharmaceutical and banking industries. These companies, in turn, have various partnerships with the U.S. government and global nongovernmental organizations (NGOs) Publicis is a partner of the World Economic Forum, which is leading the call for a "reset" of the global economy and a complete overhaul of our way of life. As such, Publicis appears to be playing an important role, coordinating the suppression of information that runs counter to the technocratic narrative

The role of the free press is to counter industry propaganda. That role has been effectively subverted through advertising. News outlets rarely report on something that might damage their advertisers

Publicis connects to the drug industry, banking industry, NewsGuard/ HealthGuard, educational institutions, Big Tech companies like Google, Microsoft and Bing, the U.S. State Department and Department of Defense, global technocratic institutions like the World Health Organization, national and global NGOs like the CCDH and the World Economic Forum, and dominating health websites like WebMD and Medscape

These connections, taken together, explain how certain views can be so effectively erased. The answer to this dilemma is transparency. We must expose the machinations that allow this agenda to be pushed forward End Quote

December 2021 Michael Rectenwald, Chief Academic Officer, American Scholars, author of "What is the Great Reset?" in Imprimis, a publication of Hillsdale College, Volume 50, Number 12, (WRL 11)

Page 1, Paragraph 1: "Is the Great Reset a conspiracy theory imagining a vast left-wing plot to establish a totalitarian one-world government? No. Despite the fact that some people may have spun conspiracy theories based on it—with some reason, as we will see—the Great Reset is real."

<u>2022</u>

Great Reset (AKA Communist Manifesto of 2020 & The Genocidal Con) read Alex Jones, *The Great Reset: And the*

War for the World

28 June 2022 Video "700 Million Worldwide Will Die from CV19 Vax by 2028 — Dr. David Martin" Greg Hunter, USA Watchdog, interviews Dr. David Martin, the top expert in the ongoing and unfolding CV19 vax genocide and litigation for 6.21.22. (WRL 12)

29 September 2022 Video "Epoch Original BORDER DECEPTION How the U.S. and U.N. Are Quietly Running the Border Crisis" Quote: America's border crisis is not organic. Behind the nearly 4.9 million illegal immigrants who entered the United States since President Joe Biden took office are criminal cartels, orchestration from the United Nations, and financing from the U.S. government. And while taxpayers are being told that local law enforcement and the National Guard are working to resolve the crisis, in reality, they're being used to funnel migrants to networks of non-governmental organizations, who then traffic them for resettlement throughout the country. End Quote (WRL 13)

4 October 2022 Article "China Installs Police Base on American Soil and Biden Does Nothing About It"

Quote: Communist China is a menace to the world of the kind that hasn't been seen since the 1930s.

The out-of-control communist police state is boosted by advanced technology and a soul-crushing ideology that caused over 100 million deaths in the 20th Century.

China has been doing its best to grow its power worldwide, including establishing naval bases around the globe, addicting Africa to cheap loans, and profiting from the devastation of the COVID virus and its hit on the U.S. economy.

Now, China is also establishing police stations on American soil. . . . More than 200,000 Chinese are currently wanted to return to China to answer for crimes. These police stations around the world are a dragnet to get them in cuffs and on a plane home.

The Chinese government monitors the lives of its citizens through telecommunications channels and closely watches everything people do and say.

This includes the social credit system where your access to loans, freedom to travel, and ability to buy a home or use basic services are affected by your loyalty to the government.

This is obviously a system that violates all human and international rights, which is what makes it all the more disturbing that globalists want to bring it to America. Beijing Biden is just a useful tool to install this creeping communism here at home. End Quote (WRL 14)

11 October 2022 Video "They're Here!" Quote: "While America Sleeps, the Chinese Communist Party Walks Right In" While Chinese-made goods flood the U.S. market, Beijing has been busy buying America—including elected officials. Even at the local level, the Chinese Communist Party (CCP) has compromised U.S. politicians as part of what it calls its subnational strategy to undermine U.S. interests. From Wall Street to Main Street and from Washington, D.C., to Small Town, USA, Beijing has infiltrated every corner of American society. And now the CCP is openly exporting its own police force to the United States to intimidate the Chinese diaspora and spy on Americans. In this shocking new episode of Over the Target, Brendon Fallon and Lee Smith reveal the massive scope of China's stealth invasion. End Quote (WRL 15)

18 October 2022 Article "CCP Acquires 96 Ports Worldwide, Experts Raise Alarm on Beijing's Ambitions" by Jenny Li

Quote: There are five in the United States, including in Miami, Houston, Long Beach, Los Angeles, and Seattle. . . . port and logistics operators handle large amounts of corporate, transport, and personal data in increasingly digitized supply chains. China may install China-made internet communications to handle the data, which could potentially enable the CCP to access local government administrations, according to Newsweek. . . . One reason for the CCP's obsession with acquiring ports in various countries is that they could serve military purposes for the regime. . . . Eyal Pinko, a former Israeli intelligence officer, in an interview with Voice of America, said that ports can easily be used to collect naval intelligence. . . . The CCP sees the Chinese ocean shipping fleets as its "moving territory" and "fortresses of warfare.". . . Along with the acquisition of ports in various countries, the CCP has been buying up land near U.S. military bases. . . . North Dakota. . . Grand Forks Air Force base, known for its top-secret drone technology. . . . Texas. . . Laughlin Air Force Base. . . . The FBI discovered that the cell towers are located near U.S. military bases in the rural Midwest, and determined that Huawei equipment atop the tower could capture and disrupt Defense Department communications, including those from the Strategic Command, which oversees U.S. nuclear weapons. End Quote (WRL 16)

22 October 2022 Video "From 'Wildfire Cancers' to Foot-Long Clots, Dr. Ryan Cole Explains the Dangers of the Spike Protein" COVID-19 mutated to Omicron variant, a virus with less lethal spike protein, yet booster vaccine shots still have Wuhan. On autopsy of stroke and heart attack victims of all ages, finding modified Wuhan spike protein from vaccine present, not the unmodified Wuhan spike protein in COVID-19. "The cells don't lie. The clots don't lie. The damaged organs don't lie. . . Cole breaks down the mechanisms by which the spike protein can cause the symptoms being reported, from brain fog to reactivated Epstein-Barr virus to changes in hormonal cycles." Interview of Dr. Ryan Cole, pathologist by Jan Jekielek. (WRL 17)

24 October 2022 Article "Newly Discovered Evidence Shows Dominion Voting 'Erroneous Code' Error Message Found in Tennessee Exists in 97% of County's System Logs Looked at in Georgia From June 2020 Through the 2022 Primary: Anomaly was thought to be isolated to just ICP tabulators. Now discovered on ICC high speed scanner in at least one county" (WRL 18)

25 October 2022 Article "It Begins: Man Gets Microchip in Hand" published StatesmanPost.com Quote: What's clear is the idea of people having chips in their hands and a future digital world currency is anything but a conspiracy: it's a coming reality. . . . The American Republic and other democratic systems are intended to put a check against tyrannical power. Though once you transform money and security into a central and controllable digital location, you put all the power into a few hands. What's even worse is this is already partly accomplished through online centralization and smartphones, where people can be locked out and have accounts shut down if they displease leaders. . . . The globalists want a one-world currency, microchipped humans, and full control. Far too many seem like they will easily go along with it. America needs to keep waking up because a lot of the rest of the world is clearly fast asleep. End Quote (WRL 19)

27 October 2022 Video "Medical Genocide: Hidden Mass Murder in China's Organ Transplant Industry/Documentary" (WRL 1)

Quote: China now performs the most organ transplants in the world, yet has few voluntary donors. While the regime has admitted to harvesting organs from death row prisoners, they account for a tiny fraction of transplants performed in the country. Based on a decade of research, this documentary uncovers the true source of these organs: an ongoing crime against humanity with an estimated tens of thousands of innocent victims each year. End Quote

In 1999 the first known victims of China's forced organ harvesting were the practitioners of Falun Gong, a spiritual/religious group that values Truthfulness, Compassion, and Tolerance. The accounts of routine blood-testing of Uyghur political prisoners and reports of mysterious deaths of Uyghurs and Tibetans in custody raised "the alarm that these populations may also be victims of involuntary organ harvesting." Visit (WRL 20) to learn more about what countries are doing to stop this (such as Israel's Organ Transplant Act in 2008 prohibiting insurance companies from reimbursing for these transplants) and who is currently being killed (mostly practitioners of Falun Gong, Uyghurs, Tibetans, and "House Christians").

24 November 2022 Video "5-Month Clot Mystery" Quote: "The clue was the embalmers. The clue was the insurance companies. The embalmers never saw anything until midway in 2021. And then they started seeing these massive clots. . . It only started six months into the vaccination program," says Steve Kirsch, the executive director of the Vaccine Safety Reseach Foundation. End Quote (WRL 21)

27 November 2022 Article "Estimated 50% of Americans Now Question Vaccine Safety" Analysis by Dr. Joseph Mercola. Quote: The culture wars that are going on in the world are really about collectivism versus individualism. The globalist cabal are desperately trying to convince countries to adopt a collectivist philosophy, which they refer to as **"prosociality,"** and move away from respect for the individual and individual rights. Nowhere is this currently more apparent than in the medical field and public health policy" End Quote (WRL 25)

SOCIALIST/COMMUNIST/GLOBALIST PLANS

Definition of globalization: "the act or process of globalizing: the state of being globalized especially: the development of an increasingly integrated global economy marked especially by free trade, free flow of capital, and the tapping of cheaper foreign labor markets" (Merriam-Webster online dictionary April 19, 2023)

Environmental, Social, and Governance (ESG) = "Enforced Socialist Governance"

Heritage Action for America (WRL 22) is leading the fight against ESG. "Under ESG, traditional American energy like oil and gas is punished and the Left's 'woke' cultural agenda is implemented from the boardroom down to the factory floor. This agenda is being pushed by green activists, woke culture warriors, global elites, and the big businesses they control." (WRL 23) Depicted on Heritage Action's online diagram of ESG hurts: Environmental includes No

Oil No Gas, Solar Subsidies, and Climate Change Disclosures; Social Includes Critical Race Theory, Pro-Abortion Policies, and Transgender Activism; Governance includes Employee Race Quotas, Compensation Tied to ESG Goals, and Social Credit Scores. 11-18-2022 Steve Warren CBN News: "G20 Leaders Agree to Global Vaccination Passport System: 'Where Will It End?'" (WRL 36) 12-5-2022 Analysis by Dr. Joseph Mercola: "An Invisible Prison Has Been Built Just for You"

Quote: Artificial Intelligence (AI) is an absolutely crucial component, without which the control system cannot work. The easiest way to push against this system is to starve AI of data by refusing to use technologies that collect and share your personal data. . . . But, as with most other technologies sold under the guise of convenience and security, facial recognition is ultimately a tool for mass control and an essential part of your individual digital prison. As explained by Jabbi, the Chinese control system is based on facial recognition in combination with a social credit system. He describes the Chinese social credit system as a feedback system that responds based on your behavior. Unbeknownst to most Westerners, an identical system has already been set in motion behind the scenes in Western countries — they just haven't told you yet. End Quote (WRL 40)

Included in Mercola's article are links to: "Must Hear Interview: Your Digital Prison Is Pretty Much Built, & Will Be The Final Lockdown" (WRL 42); "Legal Expert: European vaccine mandates are the beginning of a 'social credit system' Legal Philosopher Eva Vlaardingerbroek weighs in on Europe's vaccine mandate on 'Tucker Carlson Tonight' "(WRL 43); Twitter thread @songpinganq "Chinese government remotely switched all the protester's COVID passports to code red. . . .If you try to enter public place with a red QR code. . .Immediately an Alarm goes off. Chinese govt can easily cut you off from society By remotely switch your COVID passport to code red. . . . A green QR code needed to access to transport, food. . .even residential complex" (WRL 44); and Twitter posted by James Melville from

GingerJim "Here's a personal account of how digital ID/ central bank digital currencies/ social credit systems operate in China. Central banks and governments are nudging us towards this. We cannot let this happen. Wake up before it's too late." (WRL 45)

Transhumanism

"The Evolution of Godless Practices: Eugenics, Infanticide, and Transhumanism" Commentary by Stu Cvrk, published online by The Epoch Times Oct. 5, 2022 and Updated Oct.12, 2022. Quote: The newest effort by the godless camp to meddle with the natural course of humanity is the transhumanism movement, which seeks to accelerate "human evolution" through advanced technologies. It is a segue from eugenics because it aims to "enhance" the human species through the addition of advanced biological and physical (mechanical, bio mechanical) technologies. . . .The Biden administration has cleared the decks for transhumanism by signing the "Executive Order on Advancing Biotechnology and Biomanufacturing Innovation for a Sustainable, Safe, and Secure American Bioeconomy" on Sep.12 End Quote (WRL 24)
"Mass Monitoring: A Digital Dictatorship on the Horizon?" Analysis by Dr. Joseph Mercola on October 19, 2022 (WRL 41)

So, In Closing This Book

I turn to the best guide for the good side, the Holy Bible. From it I know that God will help us fight man's evil nature, that God can cleanse our bodies and keep us free, and that God helps those who help themselves. So I pray the Lord's Prayer in the words I learned it: "Our Father which art in Heaven, Hallowed be thy Name. Thy Kingdom come. Thy will be done in earth, As it is in heaven. Give us this day our daily bread. And forgive us our trespasses, As we forgive them that trespass against us. And lead us not into temptation, But deliver us from evil. For thine is the kingdom, The power, and the glory, For ever and ever, Amen."

About the Author

Diane Elizabeth Swanson Vann graduated with a Bachelor of Science in Nursing from the University of Nebraska Medical Center, Omaha, Nebraska in 1974 and Master of Science in Nursing from the University of Tennessee, Knoxville in 1986. She is married with no children. Her primary interests are nursing and health promotion. She is a 2019 recipient of the Marquis Lifetime Achievement Award by Marquis Who's Who, in recognition of her outstanding contributions as a nurse and nursing educator.

In an advertisement in weekly and daily newspapers January, 2010, paid for by her, in which she announced her candidacy in the Republican primary for the U.S. Congress, House of Representatives, 8th District, Georgia, she wrote "that President Obama is a run-of-the-mill communist who has cloaked himself in a 'second Messiah' kind of mystique. She recommends that Americans read for themselves the 'Communist Manifesto' or 'Manifesto of the Communist Party' written by Karl Marx in 1848 and contrast it to our 'Declaration of Independence,' the 'Constitution of the United States of America' and the 'Gettysburg Address.'" She wrote this book as an aid for fulfilling that objective.

This self published book was originally copyrighted and published by AuthorHouse on 1/6/2012 with the title How the Communist Manifesto of 1848 Blueprints the Actions of the Democratic Party and President Obama Today. The title, while transparent, proved unworkably long, so the author moved it to subtitle and had the content copyrighted and published 12/13/2012 with the new title Undermining the U.S. Constitution. The revised edition published 3/13/2015 was delivered to the Washington, DC mail boxes of U.S. House Members and Delegates on 5/8/2015 and U.S. Senators on 5/11/2015. The 2017 edition, published by both

LitFire and AuthorHouse, was the first without the word "Today" at the end of the subtitle, removed because President Obama was no longer in office. The 2019 edition, copyrighted and published by Litfire, was the first to include the dedication.

March 8, 2022 she qualified in Atlanta, Georgia to run for State Senate District 18. State redistricting based upon the 2020 population was reportedly complete. However, maps with street names were not complete nor available until March 29*. Upon going to early vote May 7, she learned that she now lived in State Senate District 25. Subsequently she was sued by the Secretary of State and summoned to a May 19 hearing in the Office of State Administrative Hearings (OSAH). She was found by the judge, fairly, to be not qualified to run. (WRL 33) (WRL 34)

March 21, 2023 addition: Multiple credible people confirmed in past year that post 2020 census redistricted maps, in shape form with street names accessible via an internet application, were available for use at the county level starting in January 2022. Why both the Democrat and Republican parties were not using those shape maps for qualifying candidates in Atlanta in March 2022 remains unexplained.

Her platform included the following positions:

Position for Amendments to Constitutions

United States Constitution
To ensure that the U.S. Supreme Court "remains an independent guardian of our rights and freedoms for future generations," I support the addition of the Keep Nine Amendment to the U.S. Constitution. Its wording is "The Supreme Court of the United States shall be composed of nine Justices." (WRL 35)

Georgia Constitution
To ensure that voting machines will be free of domestic and foreign manipulation to keep the currently elected in office (WRL3), I support the addition of an amendment to the Georgia Constitution similar to Amendment XXII in the U.S. Constitution. Its wording to be "No person shall be elected to the office of Georgia Senate or Georgia House of Representatives for more than three terms of two years."

Positions On Voting Integrity

I support the passage of language in a GA bill to make physical ballots public records, doing away with the paperless voting system. Garland Favorito, cofounder of VoterGa, a nonpartisan, 501C3 nonprofit group, that stands for voters organized for trusted election results in Georgia (WRL 29) and his team of experts showed how Georgia's election results are manipulated electronically in his March 6, 2022 presentation, streamed online at: (WRL 37). The Fulton Co. 15 point Election Manipulation Evidence can be viewed at: (WRL 38)

Position on GA Citizens Petitioning for Grand Jury

I support legislation that will remove the barriers to GA citizens petitioning for a grand jury of their neighbors to hear their concerns. Citizens are entitled to directly petition for grand juries according to the U.S. Constitution. Citizens petitioning for a grand jury to hear findings from Fulton and other counties on election manipulation are being prevented by the interposition of district attorneys, a position that came into being after the implementation of the U.S. Constitution.

As one of the two Bibb County Republican Party (BCRP) poll watchers at the Macon-Bibb Board of Elections (BOE) the week before and the day before the November 3, 2020 election, I was bothered by what I didn't see. No absentee ballots were scanned except roughly 100 that, when removed from their envelopes, were judged to need the questionable process of adjudication.

All of the rest of the thousands of absentee ballots, out of their envelopes and kept in open long white containers behind a folding screen in the early voting room with the public entrance to the BOE, must have been scanned after I and my fellow watcher left at 5PM on Monday, Nov. 2, because when my fellow watcher returned to observe the following morning (I was poll working) they were reportedly done. The two of us recorded our observations. Our affidavits and those from other BCRP poll watchers, who came and watched the Nov. 3, 2020 election recounts and January 5, 2021 Perdue-Ossoff runoff election, were eventually taken to Atlanta, to a GA Senate Committee hearing on the election. After a reported 6 1/2 hour wait, the BCRP group was turned away without being heard. They left our affidavits (original copies) there as directed. Feb. 10, 2022, because of the senate's lack of feedback, I and another BCRP member tried to petition for a grand jury at the local court house.

There we indeed met, without any question, a dead end in the district attorney's office.

Position on Georgia Senate Bills 440 and 441

For Repeal of both Senate Bill 440 — The Juvenile Justice Reform Act of 1994 and Senate Bill 441 — Mandatory Minimums of 1995
Following bullet points are cited from online source of: FACT SHEET Sentencing Legislation 2019
OVERVIEW
Senate Bill 440 — The Juvenile Justice Reform Act of 1994
Senate Bill 441 — Mandatory Minimums of 1995
Passed at the time of "get tough on crime"
Impacted the rising prison population
Bills seen by the public as being tough on crime were popular at the time
Current research and prison overcrowding show that perhaps these

policies are no longer a best practice . . . .

SB 440 - THE JUVENILE JUSTICE REFORM ACT

Any juvenile offender who is convicted of seven specific offenses will serve their time in a Department of Corrections (DOC) facility, rather than in the custody of the Department of Juvenile Justice.

Gave the superior (adult) court exclusive jurisdiction over the trial of any juvenile 13-17 years of age alleged to have committed offences known as the "Seven Deadly Sins"

Murder

Rape

Armed robbery with firearm

Aggravated child molestation

Aggravated sodomy

Aggravated sexual battery

Voluntary manslaughter

Original juvenile justice system was based on a rehabilitative model that offered treatment to young offenders

Rehabilitation was replaced by retribution in the 1990s. . . . By 2006, every state had passed a juvenile transfer law. . . .

SB 441 - MANDATORY MINIMUMS

Any offender convicted of one of the seven crimes identified in SB 440 (also known as the "Seven Deadly Sins") will serve a minimum of 10 years in prison:

If the offender was sentenced to longer than the 10-year minimum, they would not be eligible for parole at any time during that sentence

A second conviction for these offenses would result in a sentence of life without parole. . . .

MY POSITION

In spite of the subsequent passage of House Bill 1176 in 2012, House Bill 349 in 2013, Senate Bill 365 in 2014, and House Bill 310 in 2015, problems remain from SB 440 and SB441.

In 1991 Georgia had roughly 15,000 prisoners. The number in 2022 is up to 45,000, of whom roughly only 77% are parole eligible.

It is alleged that SB 441 is being used by district attorneys, not to punish serious criminals, but to punish defendants who refuse to plead guilty and forfeit their constitutional right to a trial by jury.

In any case, SB 440 and 441 should be repealed. They have failed to accomplish anything of note, other than providing a fairly constant supply of prisoners for the state's privately funded prisons.

Drafted and signed Sept. 5, 2022 for Civil Action #22-SCCV-094758 case Diane S. Vann, Plaintiff versus Georgia State Treasurer, Defendant

Voting machines were brought into Georgia as a pilot program with the expectation that counties would vote for or against their continued use. That vote was never taken.

The preparation of code for each and every candidate and election in Georgia's 159 counties is done at a central location site in the state, and then disseminated to each county for their voting machines. Up through 2018 that central location was Kennesaw State University.

The expectation is that a single vote from a constituent for a candidate receives per the code a whole number of one. Unfortunately, the code being written by the information technologist for a particular candidate may, at the behest or command of a 3rd party, be written as a percentage. For example, instead of one for a vote, they get 3/4 or 75%, while the opponent desired by the 3rd party receives 1 1/4 or 125%. Or, for example, the algorithm could be written that every 16th vote goes to the opponent. Unfortunately, there is no auditing of this lengthy code prior to, during, or after its use.

To report accumulated results to the state, the master tabulating machine in each county goes online and uses the internet. That connection to the internet is hackable. Once hacked a 3rd party can, in split seconds, alter the transmission while it is in process.

I, Diane Elizabeth Swanson Vann, ran in the Republican Party Primary for the U.S. House of Representatives in 2010 (District 08), 2014 (District 12), and 2016 (District 02). I accepted each of my 3 losses as the will of the voters. However, when I started poll working and poll watching in 2020, I began to see and learn that the assumption I made, that I lost fair and square each time, was not correct.* I now know that I, like every other candidate, is being selected or not selected by a 3rd party via the machines and not by the constituents of the state of Georgia.

If I had known that in 2010, I would not have wasted any of my hard earned savings on qualifying and campaigning for office. Thankfully, I declined campaign contributions from others.

Since each of my 3 qualifying fees was just over $5000, I am suing the state of Georgia for reimbursement of a total of $15,000.

*For voting machine vulnerabilities at their start in 2000: "A video of computer programmer Clinton Eugene Curtis testifying under oath in front of the U.S. House Judiciary claiming that he was hired by authorities to help rig the outcome of U.S. elections. Curtis told the court in 2000 that he was hired by Congressman Tom Freeny to build prototype software that would allow authorities to push the results to a 51/49 outcome if needed." (WRL 30) and (WRL 31) More information at: (WRL 27), (WRL 28), (WRL 32), (WRL 29)

Feb. 13, 2023 Civil Action No. 22-SCCV-094758
State Court of Bibb County Hearing via Zoom Call (3 people on call)

Following Argument read by Plaintiff Diane Vann, who is not an attorney:

Why to Not Dismiss Civil Action No. 22-SCCV-094758

A car manufacturer can be headquartered in Detroit, Michigan, or elsewhere, but if the faulty design of a car they built causes me injury in Georgia, I have a right to sue in Georgia courts by virtue of the car company doing business in Georgia.

The Georgia State Treasurer's office is in Atlanta. I ran for office in a different part of the State. Macon-Bibb is my center.

The State Treasurer is the office of State government with the function of obtaining money from Georgians running for office, and it is the one with the capacity to return that money.

At your order, your Honor, I believe that office is the appropriate payer for any liability damages caused by any State government office.

Following read when judge asked for anything more to add:

Running for office in the United States prior to 2000 involved just 2 parties — the candidates and the voters. People who manually handled and counted the ballots were required to take an oath to not mishandle them.

The State's pilot program of computer handling of ballots introduced a 3rd party of non-oath taking computer programmers and information technologists, answerable not to the voters but instead to the company that hired them.

Since then, both computer programmers and information technology experts have testified that the results collected and reported via machines cannot be trusted. For example, in an online presentation on the integrity of U.S. election systems on August 22, 2022, retired Air Force Colonel Shawn Smith said, quote: "My background is in Space and Missile operations and also in the operational test of Complex Computer Systems.

My last assignment in the military I was overseeing the operational testing of all defense space systems except for satellite communications, so I got a really deep exposure to what the threat looks like, particularly cyberthreats to our systems, particularly what our adversaries are doing. . . . Complex systems will never be secure or securable." (WRL 50)

And in the year 2000 computer programmer Clinton Eugene Curtis testified under oath in front of the U.S. House Judiciary that he was hired by authorities to help rig the outcome of U.S. elections. Curtis told the court in 2000 that he was hired by Congressman Tom Freeny to build prototype software that would allow authorities to push the results to a 51/49 outcome if needed. (WRL 30) and (WRL 31)

Due to COVID 19, local poll workers were dropping out. Hearing the call for people to replace them, I took the training. That is when it first came home to me that our election system was indeed compromised. In fact, I was quoted in the local newspaper (The Telegraph, Nov. 15, 2020) expressing my concern about it. Quote: "There's quite a bit of love that I have for the Constitution of the United States of America, and in order for it to be upheld and be viable and for our states to remain united, we have to follow it. Following it means we get fair elections," Vann said. End quote. I said that to the press when I was poll watching at the hand recounting of the presidential election in November 2020.

Today I realize that I qualified to run as a candidate in an unethical 3 party system, knowingly adopted by the government of the State of Georgia. Thus I believe that I, as a previously unknowing constituent, deserve the return of the money I gave the State to be on its Republican primary ballot in 2010, 2014 and 2016.

End of prepared testimony read aloud in court via Zoom call by Plaintiff, Diane Vann

February 20, 2023, following phone conversation with Judge's assistant (in which assistant expressed reluctance to open in their office any website link for fear of unsafe content) sent email to both Judge's assistant and state's defending Assistant Attorney General with following request:

"Please include, if possible, the link below and the attached PDF as support for my verbal testimony February 13, 2023."

Attached were the internet link to Col. Shawn Smith's speech and a PDF of an Affidavit done 8 April 2021 by Benjamin R. Cotton, whose credentials include "a master's degree in Information Technology Management from the University of Maryland University College," for Case No. 20-9238-CZ, State of Michigan in the Circuit Court for the County of Antrim, William Bailey Plaintiff v. Antrim County. In one dated 8 June 2021, he increased his well documented observations on problems with voting equipment (including the newer Dominion) from 12 to 17.

Per follow up phone call in February to assistant, learned email request was denied by Judge.

March 21, 2023 received in email an ELECTRONIC SERVICE COPY of filing at 4:00 PM of Judge's Order Granting Motion to Dismiss.

IN THE STATE COURT OF BIBB COUNTY
STATE OF GEORGIA

DIANE S. VANN,

    Plaintiff,

v.   CIVIL ACTION FILE 22-SCCV-094758

OFFICE OF THE STATE TREASURER,

    Defendant.

ORDER GRANTING MOTION TO DISMISS

On September 6, 2022, the Plaintiff filed this action against the Office of the State Treasurer. On November 30, 2022, the Office of the State Treasurer filed a "Special Appearance Motion to Dismiss." The Court heard the Motion on February 13, 2023. After careful consideration of the Motion, the Complaint, the arguments of the parties, and pertinent legal authority, the Court enters this Order.

The Plaintiff ran for the U.S. House of Representative in the 2010, 2014, and 2016 Republican Primaries. She alleges that in these primaries, the winning candidate was "selected by a 3rd party via the machines and not by the constituents of the state of Georgia." Therefore, she seeks reimbursement of $15,000, representing the qualifying fees she paid.

The Plaintiff's claim is against the State, and pursuant to the Constitution for the State of Georgia, the State has sovereign immunity, unless it is waived. Ga. Const. Art. I, § II ¶ IX(e). Sovereign Immunity is an issue of subject matter jurisdiction for the Court, and the Plaintiff has the burden of showing the State has waived sovereign immunity. Coosa Valley Technical College v. West, 299 Ga. App. 171 (2009).

127

The Plaintiff has failed to meet her burden on the issue of sovereign immunity. She has presented no evidence or argument to show a waiver of sovereign immunity for the claims she asserts. In her argument during the hearing, she stated, as to sovereign immunity, "I can't say anything to that."

The Court finds the Defendant has sovereign immunity on the Plaintiff's claims and concludes that it is without subject matter jurisdiction. The Court does not reach the merits of Ms. Vann's claims.

IT IS HEREBY ORDERED that the Office of the State Treasurer's Motion to Dismiss is GRANTED. The entry of this Order concludes this case in this Court, and the Clerk is authorized to close the case pursuant to O.C.G.A. §9-11-58(b).

SO ORDERED, this 21st day of March 2023.

/s/ *Jeff Hanson*
Jeff Hanson, Chief Judge
State Court of Bibb County

United States District Court, Middle District of Georgia, Macon Division

Plaintiff

Diane S. Vann

Defendant

Georgia State Treasurer
200 Piedmont Ave SE, Ste 1204 West Tower
Atlanta, GA 30334

United States Constitution Article I, Section 2 (1st paragraph)

The House of Representatives shall be composed of Members chosen every second Year by the People of the several States, and the Electors in each State shall have the Qualifications requisite for Electors of the most numerous Branch of the State Legislature.

COMPLAINT

I, Diane S. Vann, ran to become a Member of the U.S. House of Representatives three different times (2010, 2014, and 2016) with the understanding that the People of Georgia were making the choice as per the U.S. Constitution. Following my enlightening poll watching and poll working in 2020, I learned through extensive personal research that Voting Machines in use in those previous elections could change the People's choice in the interest of a third unknown party.

September 6, 2022: CIVIL ACTION 22-SCCV-094758 was filed in the State Court of Bibb County State of Georgia by myself as Plaintiff and the Georgia State

Treasurer as Defendant. I sued for the state of Georgia to reimburse me $15,000 for my 3 Republican primary ballot qualifying fees (attachment 1).

November 30, 2022: the Office of the State Treasurer filed a "Special Appearance Action to Dismiss" (attachment 2).

December 19, 2022 Plaintiff filed a "Motion to Not Dismiss" (attachment 3).

February 13, 2023: The court heard the Motion via Zoom Call with myself and the Defendant's Attorney (attachment 4).

March 21, 2023: The Order Granting Motion to Dismiss was ordered by Jeff Hanson, Chief Judge State Court of Bibb County (attachment 5).

Quote from The Order: Sovereign Immunity is an issue of subject matter jurisdiction for the Court, and the Plaintiff has the burden of showing the State has waived sovereign immunity. . . . The Plaintiff has failed to meet her burden on the issue of sovereign immunity. End Quote

September 5, 2023: Following Governor Brian Kemp's acknowledgement that Voting Machines can be hacked, taped at 8th Republican Party District Fish Fry Perry, Georgia on August 26, 2023, I visited the State Court of Bibb County with the request that CIVIL ACTION FILE 22-SCCV-094758 be reopened and that sovereign immunity for the state be waived. My request was denied.

I now respectfully request CIVIL ACTION FILE 22-SCCV-094758 be reopened in the United States District Court, Middle District of Georgia, Macon Division.

Signature *Susan S. Vann*   Date 6 September, 2023

10/30/23 plaintiff Diane S. Vann adds following to case file.

I, Diane S. Vann, ran in the Georgia Republican primary for the U.S. House of Representatives in 2010, 2014, and 2016. Since 2016 I learned about the elections being stolen since the year 2000 with Dominion's predecessors. This document includes seven underlined universal resource locator (URL) addresses to sources I would share directly via the internet if permitted by the court.

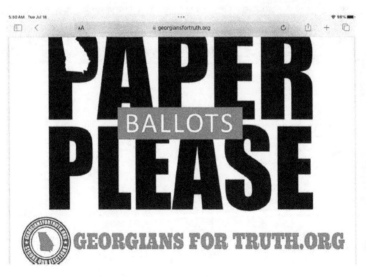

10/30/2023 EXHIBIT added to Case 5:23-cv-00340-CAR

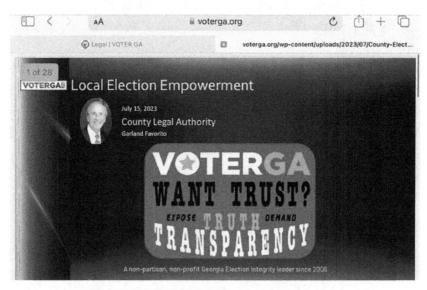

HTTPS://VOTERGA.ORG/LEGAL-ACTION/

NOTE SEQUOIA 1983 ON HTTPS://VOTERGA.ORG DIAGRAM

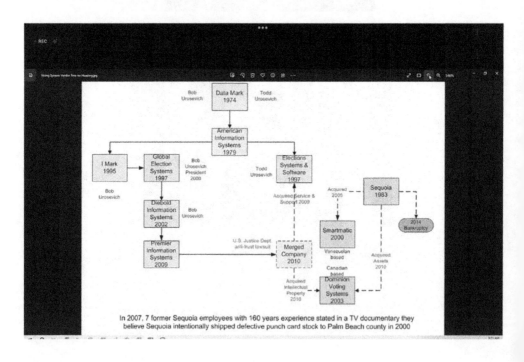

PART 1

HTTPS://DANRATHERJOURNALIST.ORG/POLITICAL-ANALYST/ELECTION-COVERAGE/2008-ELECTION/COMPILATION-2008-GENERAL-ELECTION-MATERIALS/VIDEO-

Part 2

https://www.youtube.com/watch?v=quFtd5P2Q8g&t=63s

https://rumble.com/vn49ai-murder-spies-and-voting-lies-the-clint-curtisstory.html?

● POLITICS

Video Shows Governor Brian Kemp Saying Anyone Can Hack Voting Machines, Contradictory Remarks Raise Questions

By Nimrah Khatoon · 2 months ago

A video recently surfaced on X, shedding light on an apparent contradiction in the statements of Georgia Governor Brian Kemp regarding the security of electronic voting machines used in American elections. In the video, taken during the '8th District GOP Fish Fry' event in Perry, GA on August 26th, 2023, Governor Kemp is heard discussing the inherent security vulnerabilities of electronic voting machines. This stance appears to contrast with his earlier assertions that there was no fraud in Georgia during the 2020 election, a point of contention raised by former President Trump and his team.

Uncovering the Contradiction

In the video, Governor Kemp is seen engaging with a supporter, during which he makes the candid remark, "If you give anybody a voting machine they can hack it." This statement directly contradicts his past claims that electronic voting machines used in Georgia's elections were secure and immune to hacking or tampering. These contradictory statements have ignited a debate about the credibility of assurances made by political leaders regarding the integrity of election processes.

Implications for the 2020 Election Claims

The context of Governor Kemp's contradictory remarks holds significance due to the ongoing debate over the legitimacy of the 2020 election results. President Trump and his team have consistently alleged that the election was marred by voting irregularities, particularly in states like Georgia. Governor Kemp's earlier statements dismissing claims of fraud now appear at odds with his acknowledgement of the potential security risks associated with electronic voting machines.

The Complex Landscape of Election Integrity

The contradiction in Governor Kemp's remarks underscores the complexity of discussions surrounding election integrity. While the security of electronic voting machines is a genuine concern, such technology is also subject to rigorous testing and safeguards to prevent hacking or manipulation. The issue of election security is intertwined with broader questions about public trust in the democratic process and the responsibility of leaders to provide accurate information to the electorate.

Transparency and Accountability in Politics

Governor Kemp's remarks have reignited calls for transparency and accountability in politics, particularly in matters as crucial as the integrity of elections. The discrepancy between public statements and private conversations underscores the need for elected officials to maintain consistency and honesty in their communication with the public.

The video capturing Governor Brian Kemp's candid remarks on the security of electronic voting machines presents a complex and layered narrative. As the debate over election integrity continues to unfold, this revelation prompts a reassessment of political statements, the credibility of leaders, and the responsibility of elected officials to provide accurate information to the public.

View more on Instagram

6 likes

bnnusnews

Contradiction in Georgia Governor's Statements Sparks Debate on Election Integrity 🗳️ 💬 📹

* Governor's Candid Remark: A video reveals Georgia Governor Brian Kemp acknowledging security vulnerabilities of electronic voting machines, contradicting his past assertions of their immunity to hacking or tampering.

* Impact on Election Claims: The contradiction gains significance in the context of the ongoing debate over the legitimacy of the 2020 election results, as Governor Kemp's earlier statements now appear at odds with his acknowledgment of potential security risks.

* Transparency and Trust: The incident underscores the importance of transparency and accountability in politics, highlighting the need for consistent and honest communication by elected officials on critical matters such as election integrity.

Read more:
https://bnn.network/politics/video-shows-governor-brian-kemp-saying-anyone-can-hack-voting-machines-contradictory-remarks-raise-questions/

#ElectionIntegrity #PoliticalTransparency #Accountability #PublicTrust #GovernorKemp

Add a comment...

Subscribe to BNN Breaking

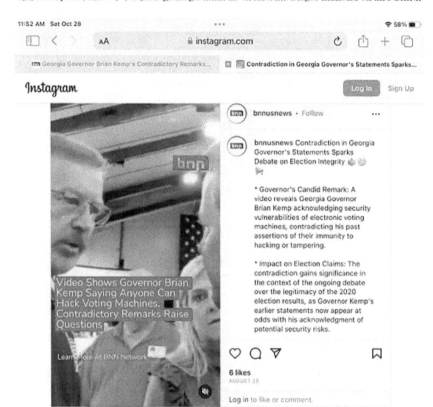

U.S. District Court [LIVE AREA]
Middle District of Georgia (Macon)
CIVIL DOCKET FOR CASE #: 5:23-cv-00340-CAR

VANN v. OFFICE OF THE STATE TREASURER GEORGIA   Date Filed: 09/08/2023
Assigned to: US DISTRICT JUDGE C ASHLEY ROYAL   Jury Demand: None
Cause: 02:437 Federal Election Commission   Nature of Suit: 190 Contract: Other
                                                     Jurisdiction: Federal Question

Plaintiff
DIANE S VANN   represented by   DIANE S VANN

V.

Defendant
OFFICE OF THE STATE   represented by   ZACHARY B JOHNSON
TREASURER GEORGIA

Date Filed	#	Docket Text
03/27/2024	9	Letter regarding Status of case (elp) (Entered: 03/28/2024)
12/15/2023	8	RESPONSE filed by DIANE S VANN re 5 MOTION TO DISMISS FOR FAILURE TO STATE A CLAIM . (elp) (Entered: 12/15/2023)
12/12/2023	7	This is a text only entry; no document issued. **ORDER** granting 6 Motion to Stay. All deadlines are STAYED pending the Court's resolution of Defendant's Motion to Dismiss for Failure to State a Claim. Ordered by U.S. DISTRICT JUDGE C. ASHLEY ROYAL on 12/12/2023. (dcb) (Entered: 12/12/2023)
12/11/2023	6	MOTION to Stay For the foregoing reasons, in the interests judicial efficiency and justice, and in order to avoid undue cost and burdens of discovery re 5 MOTION TO DISMISS FOR FAILURE TO STATE A CLAIM by OFFICE OF THE STATE TREASURER GEORGIA filed by ZACHARY B JOHNSON.(JOHNSON, ZACHARY) (Entered: 12/11/2023)
12/11/2023	5	MOTION TO DISMISS FOR FAILURE TO STATE A CLAIM by OFFICE OF THE STATE TREASURER GEORGIA filed by ZACHARY B JOHNSON.(JOHNSON, ZACHARY) (Entered: 12/11/2023)
12/01/2023	4	SUMMONS Returned Executed by DIANE S VANN as to OFFICE OF THE STATE TREASURER GEORGIA. (ggs) (Entered: 12/01/2023)
11/08/2023	3	Summons Issued as to OFFICE OF THE STATE TREASURER GEORGIA. (ggs) (Entered: 11/08/2023)
10/30/2023	2	EXHIBIT 1 - Document containing seven underlined Universal Resource Locator (URL) addresses by DIANE S VANN re 1 Complaint. (ans) (Entered: 11/08/2023)
09/08/2023	1	**COMPLAINT** against OFFICE OF THE STATE TREASURER GEORGIA filed by DIANE S VANN . Fee Paid $402, Receipt No.43265 (Attachments: # 1 Civil Cover Sheet, # 2 Letter from Diane Vann, # 3 Motion filed in state court, # 4 Objection to motion, # 5 Argument read by plaintiff, # 6 Order to Dismiss)(elp) Modified on 9/11/2023 modify docket text to add filing fee paid (elp). (Entered: 09/08/2023)

https://voterga.org/legal-action/ (VoterGA legal tab)
Curling v. Raffensperger
Included in Closing Statement Presentation Feb 2024

Dominion's Constitutional Deficiencies

Mr. Davis sought to call deposed individuals who examined Sullivan Strickler's image copy or directed tests on the Coffee County server and scanners:

 Ben Cotton – a highly credentialed cyber forensics expert not allowed to testify about remote access vulnerabilities in the Coffee server image.

 Jeff Lenberg – a nation state vulnerability testing expert with 30 years of experience at Sandia National Labs not allowed to testify about real-time remote changes affecting ballot rejections.

The record shows corroborating evidence of remote wireless access by Dominion personnel during the 2021 U.S. Senate runoff to correct a ballot rejection issue.

Curling v. Raffensperger

You Cannot Check Your Vote

Dr. Appell stated in rebuttal *"The consensus among experts is to use hand marked paper ballots and scanners because if scanners don't tabulate correctly, we can always just count the ballots."*

Georgians cannot count cast ballots because the Defendants actively oppose sunshine for those ballots even to the extent of filing an amicus court brief to keep them sealed.

After 3 years and a GA Supreme Court win, the public is still unable to detect how many Fulton Co. counterfeit ballots there were, nor verify their dubious electronic results.

Dr. Gilbert summed up Georgia's election transparency problem when he stated, *"You can check your bank account but not your vote."*

Curling v. Raffensperger

141

Quotation from Wikipedia 10 April 2024

"Justice delayed is justice denied" is a legal maxim. It means that if legal redress or equitable relief to an injured party is available, but is not forthcoming in a timely fashion, it is effectively the same as having no remedy at all. . . . Martin Luther King Jr., used the phrase in the form "justice too long delayed is justice denied"

https://en.wikipedia.org/wiki/Justice_delayed_is_justice_denied

Dedication

This book is dedicated to my beloved only sibling, Karen Imogene Swanson. Karen was born September 5, 1948 in Sidney, Nebraska. She walked at 2 years of age instead of the expected 1 year, and she talked at 4 years instead of the expected 2. Almost 4 years old when I was born, Mother taught us together how to tie our shoes and tell time. Smart in her way, I did not guess she was a slow learner until I was 11 years old and our parents asked me to help her with her math. In 1969 she graduated from Niles McKinley High School, Niles, Ohio, reading and functioning at the level of a 12 year old according to her special education teacher. Karen had an amazing memory for names and dates, loved to read, do jumbles, and care for our pets.

Karen never experienced menses, any breast development or other signs of puberty, and, unlike the rest of the family, she was short. In 1981 medical science progressed to the point where chromosomes could be seen and counted, so I, a registered nurse, took her to see a geneticist. Karen was diagnosed with Classic Turner's Syndrome. Karen had 45 instead of 46 chromosomes in every cell. She was missing her second sex chromosome. The doctor explained that while she was born a girl, at puberty her ovaries failed to mature and her bone growth abruptly slowed leaving her with fragile bones. He predicted 2 changes that did eventually occur, the growth of skin moles and deafness.

Although Karen wept initially at each of her life's limitations, she accepted them matter of factly and carried on with a positive, independent spirit. She always did the most with what she had, inspiring everyone who knew her to do the same. April 28, 2018 Karen ended her day in Macon, Georgia with her usual smile and nod. Looking for her the next morning, I found her stiff in bed, on her right side in the fetal position, with her hands together in the praying position pointed toward her chin. Certainly, as my Karen was an angel on Earth, she is now an angel in Heaven.

Recommended Reading and References

W. Cleon Skousen, _The Naked Communist_, (Salt Lake City: Ensign Publishing Company, 1958) Library of Congress Catalog Card Number: 58-14464.

K. Carl Smith with Dr. Karnie C. Smith, Sr., _Frederick Douglass Republicans: The Movement to Re-Ignite America's Passion for Liberty_, (Bloomington: Authorhouse, 2011) ISBN: 978-1-4567-5814-1 (e), Library of Congress Control Number: 2011905012.

Grace-Marie Turner, James C. Capretta, Thomas P. Miller, Robert E. Moffit, _Why Obamacare Is Wrong For America: How the New Health Care Law Drives Up Costs, Puts Government in Charge of Your Decisions, and Threatens Your Constitutional Rights_, (New York: HarperCollins, 2011) ISBN: 978-0-06-207601-4.

Joseph Katz, ed., _The Communist Manifesto, Karl Marx and Friedrich Engels; the Revolutionary Economic, Political, and Social Treatise That Has Transfigured the World_, (New York: Pocket Books, 1964) ISBN: 13: 978-0-671-67881-4 and 10: 0-671-67881-7.

Rius, _Marx For Beginners_, (New York: Pantheon Books, 1979) ISBN: 0-375-71461-8.

Jonathan Hennessey, Aaron McConnell, _The United States Constitution: A Graphic Adaptation_, (New York: Hill and Wang, 2008) ISBN: 13:978- 0-8090-9470-7 and 10: 0-8090-9470-3.

Charlotte Thomson Iserbyt, _The Deliberate Dumbing Down of America: A Chronological Paper Trail_, (Ravenna: Conscience Press, 1999) ISBN: 0-9667071-0-9, Library of Congress Catalog Card Number: 98–89726.

Author(s) United Nations Conference On Environment & Development Rio De Janerio, Brazil, 3 To 14 June 1992, _Agenda 21: Earth Summit: The United Nations Programme of Action from Rio_, (Copyright United Nations Division for Sustainable Development; in its current format and edits is Copyright CrabCube, Inc 2013)

ISBN-13: 978-1482672770 and 1482672774.

Dr. Ileana Johnson Paugh, *U.N. Agenda 21: Environmental Piracy,* ISBN: 0615716474 and 13: 978-0615716473.

Freedom Advocates Recognize Unalienable Rights, *Understanding Sustainable Development -- Agenda 21: For the People and their Public Officials,* online PDF White Paper and PDF Pamphlet revised 2004, 2005, 2007, and 2010.

Tom DeWeese and Contributors, *Agenda 21: The Wrenching Transformation of America*, 3rd ed. (Virginia: American Policy Center, 2016), americanpolicy.org/manual.

Alex Jones, *The Great Reset: And the War for the World,* (Skyhorse Publishing, 2022) ISBN: 978-1-5107-7404-9.

Andrew C. McCarthy, "Hamas Operatives Are Not 'Militants.' They Are Jihadists" (National Review Oct. 10, 2023)
https://www.nationalreview.com/2023/10/hamas-operatives-are-not-militants-they-are-jihadists/

Stephen Coughlin, *Catastrophic Failure: Blindfolding America In the Face of Jihad,* (North Charleston, SC: CreateSpace Independent Publishing Platform, 2015) ISBN: 13:978-1511617505, Library of Congress Control Number: 2015905620.

William Gawthrop, Ph.D. *The Criminal Investigator-Intelligence Analyst's Handbook of Islam,* (Outskirts Press, Inc., 2021) Paperback ISBN: 9781977243010. Hardback ISBN: 9781977243027.

"Everything You Need to Know about the Government's Mass Censorship Campaign." Interview of Mike Benz, Executive Director of Foundation for Freedom Online, by Tucker Carlson 16 Feb 2024. https://www.youtube.com/watch?v=CRYSKaS-XtQ

Matthew J. Trewhella, *The Doctrine of the Lesser Magistrates: A Proper Resistance to Tyranny and a Repudiation of Unlimited Obedience to Civil Government,* (CreateSpace Independent Publishing Platform, North Charleston, South Carolina, 2013) ISBN:1482327686 and 13: 9781482327687, Library of Congress Control Number: 2013902222.

WEBSITE REFERENCE LIST (WRL)

Detailed citations for references are available in the printed format of this book. Because of the dynamic nature of the Internet, any web addresses or links may have changed since publication and may no longer be valid. Or, because web addresses in print may get moved to fit the page, they may contain a blank, empty space or spaces. Omitting those spaces when entering the address onto the Internet may bring success.

And, the same web addresses may go and return. Example: The Epoch Times video "Behind the Push for Open Borders" by Trevor Loudon (WRL 5) was posted at dianevann.com (WRL 26) in 2020. Its lack of connection was "first noted 2021 February 14." The same link resumed working months later in 2021.

1. page 113 (WRL 1)
https://www.theepochtimes.com/medical-genocide-hidden-mass-murder-in-chinas-organ-transplant-industry-documentary_4817370.html

2. page 89 (WRL 2)
https://www.youtube.com/watch?v=r9-3K3rkPRE

3. page 119 (WRL 3)
https://rumble.com/v2fon92-mark-cooks-first-real-time-demonstration-of-flipping-votes.html

4. page 104 (WRL 4)
https://globallibertymedia.com/fascism-was-socialism-2-0/

5. page 106 (WRL 5)
https://www.facebook.com/epochtimes/videos/2132019683512986/?_so_=serp_videos_tab

6. page 106 (WRL 6)

https://thenewamerican.com/bilderberg-meeting-2019-nothing-to-see-here-move-along/

7. page 107 (WRL 7)

https://www.thegatewaypundit.com/2020/04/dr-fauci-gave-3-7-million-wuhan-laboratory-something-going-rudy-giuliani-drops-bomb-niaid-director-dr-tony-fauci/

8. page 108 (WRL 8)

https://summit.news/2020/12/01/firm-that-owns-dominion-voting-systems-received-400-million-from-swiss-bank-with-connection-to-chinese-government-before-election/

9. page 108 (WRL 9)

https://greatreset.com/

10. page 108 (WRL 10)

https://www.bitchute.com/video/Xb4aF6QQIrhT/

11. page 109 (WRL 11)

https://imprimis.hillsdale.edu/what-is-the-great-reset/

12. page 110 (WRL 12)

https://rumble.com/v1acoaa-up-to-100-million-will-die-from-cv19-vax-by-2028-dr-david-martin.html

13. page 110 (WRL 13)

https://www.theepochtimes.com/border-deception-how-the-us-and-un-are-quietly-running-the-border-crisis_4751511.html?

14. page 111 (WRL 14)

https://www.freshoffthepress.org/china-installs-police-base-on-american-soil-and-biden-does-nothing-about-it/

15. page 111 (WRL 15)

https://www.theepochtimes.com/while-america-sleeps-the-chinese-communist-party-walks-right-in_4789896.html?

16. page 112 (WRL 16)

https://www.theepochtimes.com/ccp-acquires-96-ports-worldwide-experts-raise-alarm-on-beijings-ambitions_4802913.html

17. page 112 (WRL 17)

https://www.theepochtimes.com/from-wildfire-cancers-to-foot-long-clots-dr-ryan-cole-explains-the-dangers-of-the-spike-protein_4813813.html?utm_source=ai&utm_medium=search

18. page 112 (WRL 18)

https://canncon.substack.com/p/newly-discovered-evidence-shows-dominion

19. page 113 (WRL 19)

https://www.statesmanpost.com/it-begins-man-gets-microchip-in-hand/

20. page 113 (WRL 20)

https://www.chinaorganharvest.org/

21. page 114 (WRL 21)

https://www.theepochtimes.com/this-has-cost-millions-of-lives-steve-kirsch-on-suppression-of-repurposed-drugs-and-a-spike-in-deaths-5-months-after-vaccine-rollout_4882569.html

22. page 114 (WRL 22)

https://heritageaction.com/

23. page 114 (WRL 23)
https://esghurts.com/

24. page 116 (WRL 24)
https://www.theepochtimes.com/the-evolution-of-godless-practices-eugenics-infanticide-and-transhumanism_4770494.html?utm_medium=email&utm_

25. page 114 (WRL 25)
https://www.bitchute.com/video/9HHOOhNU5l9m/

26. page 108 (WRL 26)
https://dianevann.com/Links.html

27. page 108, 123 (WRL 27)
https://frankspeech.com/tv/video/absolute-proof-exposing-election-fraud-and-theft-america-enemies-foreign-and-domestic

28. page 123 (WRL 28)
https://defendingtherepublic.org

29. page 119, 123 (WRL 29)
https://voterga.org/

30. page 104, 123, 125 (WRL 30)
https://rumble.com/vn1ihu-computer-programmer-testifies-that-congressman-tom-feeny-tried-to-pay-him-t.html

31. page 104, 123, 125 (WRL 31)
https://www.electionsatrisk.org/clips/computer_programmer.shtml

32. page 123 (WRL 32)
https://eternalvigilance.us/

33. page 118 (WRL 33)

https://macon-newsroom.com/13478/news/midstate-candidate-disqualified-to-run-in-georgia-senate-race/

34. page 118 (WRL 34)

https://www.youtube.com/watch?v=l8VBAMwOYzA&t=1s

35. page 118 (WRL 35)

https://keepnine.org/

36. page 115 (WRL 36)

https://www1.cbn.com/cbnnews/world/2022/november/g20-leaders-agree-to-global-vaccination-passport-to-limit-rights-of-travelers-where-will-it-end

37. page 119 (WRL 37)

https://rumble.com/vwmwup-VoterGA-press-conference-March-7th.html

38. page 119 (WRL 38)

https://voterga.org/wp-content/uploads/2022/03/Press-Release-VoterGA-2020-Fulton-Election-Results-Manipulated-03-07-22.pdf

39. page 108 (WRL 39)

https://www.weforum.org/focus/the-great-reset

40. page 115 (WRL 40)

https://articles.mercola.com/sites/articles/archive/2022/12/05/invisible-prison-digital-id.aspx?

41. page 116 (WRL 41)

https://takecontrol.substack.com/

42. page 115 (WRL 42)

https://www.youtube.com/watch?v=TgbNku6aAWY

43. page 115 (WRL 43)

https://www.foxnews.com/video/6292487785001

44. page 115 (WRL 44)

https://twitter.com/songpinganq/status/1595456780557062144

45. page 116 (WRL 45)

https://twitter.com/JamesMelville/status/1597282329181159425?s=20&t=zIZ-iNqfQq6FblcG61_uP0A

46. page 103 (WRL 46)

https://www.archives.gov/files/federal-register/executive-orders/pdf/12852.pdf

47. page 103 (WRL 47)

https://dianevann.com/Agenda-21.html

48. page 107 (WRL 48)

https://rumble.com/vdxdfb-americas-frontline-doc-tors-1st-summit-washington-dc-july-27-2020.html

49. page 107 (WRL 49)

https://rumble.com/vc3nld-dr.-immanuel-said-it-all-do-not-take-the-vaccines.html

50. page 125 (WRL 50)

https://frankspeech.com/video/ret-col-shawn-smith-speaks-moment-truth-summit

51. page 40 (WRL 51)

https://en.wikipedia.org/wiki/Year_Without_a_Summer

52. page 40 (WRL 52)

https://www.prageru.com/video/whats-wrong-with-wind-and-solar
https://www.prageru.com/video/a-world-without-fossil-fuels

www.ingramcontent.com/pod-product-compliance
Lightning Source LLC
Jackson TN
JSHW022046151224
75420JS00001B/89